T0146671

Pastor! Pastor!

Katie S. Watson

authorHOUSE®

AuthorHouse™
1663 Liberty Drive
Bloomington, IN 47403
www.authorhouse.com
Phone: 1 (800) 839-8640

Published by AuthorHouse 06/13/2018

ISBN: 978-1-5462-4172-0 (sc)
ISBN: 978-1-5462-4171-3 (e)

Library of Congress Control Number: 2018905661

Print information available on the last page.

DEDICATION

Dedicated with love to the memory of
Rev. Gilbert Hinton Watson; passing from
this life to glory, May 13, 1992. Sorely
missed by wife, Katie; his 7 children; 20
grandchildren; 30 great grandchildren.

'God testifying of his gifts; and by it he
being dead yet speaketh.' Hebrews 11:4

****

Pandora's box of memories, shadowy
detritus of your lives. Glimpses of your
early years, our love, our joy, our strife.

When loneliness pursues me, I root among
its fold. Reliving ancient moments, walking lanes of tales retold.

Awesome God!

The gift of recollection, resurrection of pleasures old. Will
one day be redundant, as we walk those streets of gold.

Love, Katie

Rev. Gilbert Hinton Watson
Departed in this life
May 13, 1992
Sorely missed by his wife, 5 sons and 2 daughters

It won't be long; it cannot be
The signs are everywhere
Of the soon returning King of Kings
And his meeting in the air.
I'll know you then, though it's been
Year; Since last I saw your face.
We'll join the soaring saints of God
Singing Amazing, Amazing Grace.

Katie

Dedicated to:

Grandchildren: Faith, Timothy G. II, Danny, Jeannie, Phillip II, Alex, Scott, Neil, Stephanie, Cameron, Hamilton, Grayson, April, Ashley, Jack Phillip, Mark II,Valerie, Cathy, Stephen, Timothy, A,

Great Grand Children: Timothy C, Trevor, Brittany, Trey, Katlyn, Cara, William, Maggie, Mollie, Alison, Gretchen, Robert, Alex, Andrew, Aiden, Maureen, Greyson, Gentry, Gaia, Ocean, Sarah, Jennifer, Katie, Moira, Hannah, Hallie, Sawyer, Kamryn Natalie

and my 1st Great, Great Grand Child Almetta Faith

Indebted to the following:

Alicia , for her untiring help in putting Pastor-Pastor with her computer knowledge, proof reading and content consistency

Nick and Beverley: For the Video Eye

Mary and Becky, my daughters for their encouragement and help

Carrie, my granddaughter in law for her excellent editing

Thomas, my son for artwork

Phil and Maureen, Son and daughter- in- law for handling the submission of the book

Great-Great Granddaughter, Great Grandchildren, Grandchildren & Children

CHAPTER ONE

Ring, ring!

Three a.m.? This has to be serious, he surmised, reaching for his bedside phone. "Pastor Davenport here. Who is call...."

"Pastor! Pastor! Ed's got a gun, locked himself in the bathroom, and threatening to commit suicide."

"Have you called 911, Molly?"

Silence. "Well, no. I'd rather keep it quiet, Pastor. Ed'll be real, real embarrassed when he comes to his senses, if I call anyone but you."

"Mmmm," sighed Pastor Robert Davenport; Bert to all who felt comfortable using that moniker. "Does he say why he wants to commit suicide...this time, Molly?"

Heavy sighing from the other end of the line. "Well, yeah; says the Spirit's left him and he's depressed. Wants to end it all...find out where his soul's gonna end up. He's real, real confused, Pastor, real, real confused." Sigh.

"I'm on my way, Molly. Tell him to wait till I get there before he pulls the trigger, so I can pray for his departing soul."

A sigh of relief found its way to Davenport's ears as he shook his head wearily.

"Thanks, Pastor. I knew I could count on you. You've got the patience of Job."

Yeah, thought Bert Davenport, pulling his trousers over his pajama bottoms. And it's about time I got around to preaching that old Job was anything but patient; anyone reading past chapter three finds that out. Bert was arguing with himself as he headed for the Brown's domicile. Hopefully, he grinned mischievously, Ed stays in the bathroom till their kids wake up and need to use the toilet. That'll get him movin' on out.

Cracked cups sat on the kitchen table waiting for Molly Brown to pour in delicious smelling coffee. Ed, a lump of a man, hair and stubble prematurely gray, sat head in hands, elbows resting on the wooden table. Lisa, their 16-year-old, had awakened, pounded on the bathroom door demanding entrance. "Daddy, if I don't get in, I'll embarrass myself in the hall." Hearing the cry of his oldest child was all it took to get Ed, and his empty gun, out of the bathroom.

"Dunno what came over me, Bert. Could chalk it up to stress at work... the talk 'bout layoffs, or could've been feeling helpless trying to keep up with the needs of the kids. You know...shoes, coats; winter comin' on. I dunno, something snapped when the word got round the plant today that the oldest guys were gonna get the axe first. Where am I gonna find work at my age these days?" He looked over at Bert for answers.

Davenport looked at the big, rough, gnarled hands that'd worked for years in a lumber yard; pity mixed with compassion swept over the pastor. What had he to offer that would mitigate these concerns? Nothing concrete. His specialty was solving problems of the Spirit, relying on promises in the Bible. But there were times when a man needed to SEE— not just HOPE—that things would change. He left reverie to listen to what Ed was saying.

"But, Pastor, I shoulda known better than to scare Molly like that." He reached over and patted his wife's hand. Molly smiled weakly at her husband; the scare was gone, but concern lingered on.

"Life's tough," agreed Bert, searching desperately for the right words. "But, hey, you're part of our church family. We won't see your family go without. You know that, Ed."

"Yeah, I know Bert, but I never was one to have my hand out; always did the best I could for me and mine."

Bert nodded, but also knew the workers in the church pantry and clothes closet were always on the lookout for Ed's kids. They didn't make a song and dance of the church's help, especially knowing Ed's makeup. The pastor sat back on the wooden chair and cleared his throat. "You know Ed, it's times like these that I'd like to be able to part the waters. But being human, that's not going to happen. Miracles are God's department. If I could, I'd have the president of your company write a personal letter guaranteeing you a job there for life."

Ed looked up and grinned. "Yeah, I hear you Bert. That would be nice, not to have to worry about my job."

A shift in mood was all Bert needed to don his pastor hat. "Yeah, Ed," he said solemnly. "Then you could leave God out of the job picture; not need His help? But me, Ed, I need God's help in everything connected with my life." He took a sip of Molly Brown's delicious coffee and continued. "I get flummoxed, Ed, when my people are in deep trouble and look to me to drum up answers. Like now, I shouldn't be wasting my gray cells worrying about your situation. I should be praying to God to wake you up, remind you that He knows your situation and He is already working on it. Right now, you're worried about your job, right?" Ed nodded. "Have you gotten a pink slip telling you you're going to be laid off?"

"Well, no...but the guys round me got info from somebody with connections, that layoffs are in the works. They're all scared like me."

"OK, OK. I get it. But Ed, 'till you actually are pink slipped, it's only a rumor. Right?"

"Well. Yeah...I guess...."

"So you want to cash in on life on a rumor?"

Ed was silent, took a gulp of coffee, held up the cup to Molly and grinned at Bert. "Kinda stupid, right Bert?"

"You got it! So let's pray that it doesn't happen, and if it does, God has another job out there with your name on it. OK?" Ed grinned sheepishly and nodded.

"Let's pray," said a relieved Rev. Davenport. "Dear God, give us the faith to believe that what we deem impossible, you're already working out for our good. Help us to take courage from the words of the Psalmist who proclaimed, 'What time I am afraid I will trust in Thee.' Help Ed to take comfort in the knowledge that You are in control of every aspect of his life. You know the needs of his family, know his concern for their welfare as head of the house. Help him to turn to You rather than to fear when he gets anxious. In Jesus' name we pray. Amen."

"You know Ed, all of us at one time or another, forget that God owns the cattle on a thousand hills, the wealth in every mine. We forget God's provisions for His children are limitless. His concern, unfathomable. We might not be able to see the money in the bank, but when we need it, God's going to be there supplying it in His own unique way."

"You're a good man, Bert Davenport," said a tearful Ed Brown, wiping his eyes with his large paw. "We're lucky to have you for our preacher."

Molly refilled their mugs with hot coffee. Bert held his out to Ed, the cups meeting in midair. "Here's to a better future," said the Rev. Robert Davenport as they clinked coffee cups.

Ed beamed and Molly Brown wiped away tears and said, "Amen."

Ed saw him to the door, paused, and put his big calloused hand on Bert's shoulder. "You're one in a million Pastor, you've seen us through thick and thin. God bless you and keep you with us till God calls you home."

Bert reflected on the longevity inference, and wondered if he were ready to stay or ready to go...and from whence? On the way home he remembered conversations he and Jenny had had about the "Brown menagerie" as some parishioners uncharitably dubbed the family. "Molly's like a deck of cards with a couple cards missing," Bert said jokingly to Jenny one time. "You're right dear," Jenny retorted. "But if Molly weren't a bit thick she just might be the queen of clubs rather than the queen of hearts she is now." "Good analogy," Bert had said, remembering his late wife's portrait of Molly Brown, as he entered his driveway.

Jenny had made sure the women working in the church's Clothes Closet kept Molly Brown's kids in mind, especially at the change of seasons. They were family, regulars in church and Sunday school; not like some who showed up for a handout but never darkened the church door till another crisis arose. Bert turned restlessly in bed, thinking of the evening with the Browns. He was seldom called on for counseling these days. Traditional or historical Christianity was slowly being replaced with the social gospel mystique. Psychiatrists and psychologists were replacing pastoral counseling. The church no longer set the standard for moral conduct; liberalism set the tone instead.

Chapter Two

The office door slammed as the indignant chairman of the board of deacons made his exit from the pastor's study. Bert watched Bob go; rigid back, outrage following in his wake. What was going on? Billingsly had always consulted him before launching anything that involved the pulpit. "I'm getting too old for surprises, Bob...well intentioned or not. Maybe I'm too territorial. But if I'm not careful, goodness knows who or what could pop up behind the pulpit one Sunday morning."

Bert leaned his head back on the headrest of his brown leather chair, and swung from side to side, thinking, wondering, and second guessing. Had he been too harsh with his deacon? He reasoned aloud to himself. "Maybe I've run my course; maybe it's time for me to get out of Dodge... let the church get a preacher who's comfortable with new ideologies and 21st century lifestyle. But I can't cut tradition and historical facts from my sermons. One day I'll stand before God to give an account of my stewardship. How do you think God will respond to my plea? 'God, I couldn't tell them about Jesus and the Cross; it was too bloody and offensive for millennial ears.'"

Bert argued with himself; the Spirit never gave him a pass to disregard his oath of fidelity to God to preach the gospel of salvation to the multitude. Everyone died; everyone would stand before their Maker. He was tired, disillusioned; the drumbeat to change church services from traditional to contemporary, progressive, was cropping up more and more. The head deacon had caught him off guard. His eyes rested on the silver framed portrait of Jenny. He bent forward, picked up the frame, and sighed heavily. "Honey, I could sure use your wisdom right now. We're going for a split; I'm glad you're not around to fret over it."

A gentle knock rescued him from maudlin melancholia.

"Come in."

Alice Morgan, secretary, office manager, and factotum of every wish from pastor to congregation, entered, carrying a tray with coffee and a muffin on a plate. She put it on his desk and remarked, "Thought you might need this, Pastor...after Bob."

Bert grinned. "Yeah, Alice, right as usual. Get yourself a coffee, we need to talk." She left and returned with coffee and a napkin carrying a muffin, and sat across from him, sipping coffee and waiting.

Alice was every wife's dream of a perfect secretary. Alice was colorless, bulky, unattractive. Wives lost no sleep over hankie pankie at the office once they met Alice. She wore no makeup, had hair the color of mud, cut as if by garden shears, that covered forehead to eyebrows. Her clothes hung like sackcloth on a shapeless body. Horned-rimmed glasses hid most of her face. In a church setting, she added nothing to office gossip. "The preacher and his secretary? Are you blind? Nothing there for any guy to lust after, let alone our preacher."

Robert Davenport stopped enjoying his muffin and remarked, "You know what Bob was here about?"

Alice nodded. "Oh yes, he ran it past me before coming in to see you. The deacons have invited a Dr. Reginald Faulkner to speak to our congregation three weeks from Sunday morning. Did you know about this, Pastor?"

Bert took a gulp of coffee, swallowed it, and put down his cup hard and shook his head. "That's the rub, Alice. They invite this important guy, move me from my pulpit to a front row pew, without so much as a 'by your leave, Pastor.' Maybe I'm too possessive of my pulpit, but after standing behind it for over 18 years, I kinda thought I had first dibs on who stood behind it. Maybe possession isn't nine-tenths of the law for pulpits anymore." Bert resumed eating his muffin and drinking coffee. Suddenly he began to laugh. "Alice, I told him to call the deacon board, arrange to meet in my office at 7 p.m. tomorrow night. Then we could discuss this up-and-coming event in detail." He grinned at her. Alice waited for his humor to subside.

Bert smiled, mischief in his eyes. "Alice, the deacons are good men... well, some I'd rather see the whites of their eyes than turn my back on. But they've never put a meeting together from scratch. I'm betting they're going to be in shock when I list the things they'll have to do to get Dr. Faulkner's meeting off the ground. Too many liberal-minded people have a propensity for dreaming up great ideas, then assigning the carrying out of those brilliant plans to underlings. Of course they take credit for the finished product, if it's a success. Verbiage to liberals is all that's necessary; it's always someone else that does the real work.

"The deacons see this event as the beginning of a great revival in our church. And, it may well be...but the onus of responsibility for getting this grand event off the ground, is going to be strictly theirs. It's their baby and they'll have to feed and change it as needed.

"I sound childish and uncharitable Alice, but this schism could have been avoided if the matter had been handled according to our church law. The pastor has control of the pulpit—until they vote him out of office. Which may be their intent," he added, tongue in cheek. Bert shrugged; Alice winced at his words. She was aware of such gossip floating around the church.

"I would probably have acquiesced to their request to invite this speaker, whom they feel the congregation will greatly benefit from his message. And in spite of my pique, I want Dr. Faulkner to be given the respect due him. My conscience would haunt me if I didn't pray for the meeting to be a success. I regret I will not have an opportunity to meet him before he preaches; apparently he will arrive in Safe Haven early Sunday morning. I'd like to hear his take on what is happening in mainline churches today; that's his area of expertise."

Bert finished his coffee, sat back in his chair and closed his eyes. He was tired, physically and mentally. His gut was in knots. There was something more involved than hearing an evangelist give a speech on changes going on in traditional churches. The church gossips were shouting from the housetops, "Isn't it time we changed pastors?"

"Anything I can do, Pastor?" Alice's voice brought him back from his meanderings.

"Sorry, I didn't mean to ignore your presence, but yeah there is. I want your advice. Should we serve coffee tomorrow night?"

Alice thought of the time when, as office manager, she'd taken care of details related to office conferences. She shook her head. "Inasmuch as disagreements could arise, serving coffee could be seen as placating ruffled feathers. So, no, I wouldn't serve coffee. Under convivial circumstances, yes, we'd serve coffee."

Bert looked at her and nodded. "Never thought coffee could be viewed as a weakness, but you're right. Now, should we ask the congregation to bring food for a potluck meal after the morning service, for Faulkner?"

She demurred a bit longer then shook her head. "We had a potluck dinner three weeks ago. Potlucks can become tedious. People might stay home if they resent bringing another covered dish."

"You amaze me, Alice. I believe Jenny would have given me the same advice. Remind me to tell John Folk to add a bit to your salary." Alice colored and shook her head. "And Alice," he went on, "I want Treasurer Folk there when I raise the question of an honorarium. See how that plays out in Peoria." He grinned at her; she grinned back, and nodded.

Bert looked at his watch: 5:45. "Hey, time we got outta here; sorry I kept you so long."

"No matter, I've nothing planned." Alice gathered the cups and food detritus and headed for the door.

"Alice," Bert said suddenly. "How about us grabbing a bite to eat? Could be I've forgotten something about tomorrow night. We could meet at Charlie's if that's OK with you."

Alice knew it was just a casual invitation but she was thrilled at the thought of eating in a restaurant with Bert. She'd been in love with him since watching the tender care he'd given his dying wife. He had joked with Jennie, carried her when she could no longer walk, teased her into eating just a morsel. Alice dreaded the thought that he might find out her feelings for him. If that happened she knew she'd have to find other employment. "Yes, Charlie's is fine. I'll see you there."

Awkwardness sat in the booth between them. Casual morning coffee claques in Bert's office were missing, replaced with a search for something to focus on. Bert was acutely aware of the tension. Alice found it difficult to look over at him. A waitress relieved the tension.

"Coffee for two?"

They said yes in unison. She left them perusing menus, another reprieve, while they dealt with the discomfort that had risen between them.

Back with coffees, the waitress asked if they were ready to order, and looked at Alice. Alice nodded. "I'll have soup and half of a chicken salad sandwich on whole wheat toast. Thanks."

"What kind of soup are we talking about?" Bert asked.

"Chicken noodle," the waitress replied.

He shrugged. "That sounds OK. I'll have soup and make my sandwich ham, on white bread, not toast. Thank you." He gave her both menus and looked at Alice, pleased that he finally was in control of his floundering emotions. Alice smiled back. Tension made its exit, to their relief.

As they waited for their orders, Bert discussed the deacon meeting scheduled for the next evening. "I think we should get in touch with Scott Martin...ask him to attend. Something I'm bringing up will involve him."

Alice nodded. "I'll call him first thing in the morning." Their meals appeared; grace was said; they ate in amicable friendship.

"Jenny said you'd come from up North." Alice nodded.

"Never lived up there; visited a few times, but shoveling snow never became a passion I wanted to acquire." He grinned sheepishly.

She laughed. "Right! The snow gets pretty deep in New York. But shoveling snow was never one of my chores. Driving in snow is tricky. But most New Yorkers use subways to move around; more convenient. Traffic's horrendous; not many drive cars to work."

"So what brought you south; and why to our city? Jenny said you were looking for a haven, that's why you stopped here at Safe Haven. That right?"

Alice nodded and looked down at her empty soup bowl.

"Sorry, but this preacher's curious about all his parishioners. My calling is to help not only the spiritual, but as is humanly possible, emotional needs as well. You're an enigma, Alice. At times I've seen fear engulf you, especially if an unknown male comes into my office. You freeze up and don't relax until the reason for their coming is stated. Are you still running from the person you told Jenny about, when you applied for this job? I've wanted to ask, but the opportunity never presented itself. This is as good a time as any to unburden yourself. By now you know how much counseling I do."

Bert took a bite of his sandwich and waited for her to digest what he'd offered. He knew by facial expressions that she was mulling over his statement. He swallowed his food and picked up his coffee cup, and motioned to the passing waitress. She obliged; topped both coffees and left.

"Airing a problem is sensible and healthy. If I'm overstepping pastoral boundaries, I apologize. But I would be less than honest if I did not say you cannot continue to run. Running is never the answer."

Alice took off her glasses, laid them on the table, and rubbed her eyes. She pushed her mousy hair back from her forehead and considered her options. Did she want him to know her sordid past? It surprised her that Bert had been aware of her apprehension each time a strange man entered the office. She'd been afraid one of George's goons had finally located her. Her fears were escalating; she saw stalkers in every man that stopped outside her small apartment. How long could she go on looking over her shoulder? Perhaps this was the time to talk, discuss her anxieties. Why not confide in her pastor?

Bert watched her remove her glasses and push back her hair from her forehead. He blinked rapidly. Without those horrid specs, and hair falling over her eyes, Alice was a good-looking woman.

When she reached to put them back on, Bert's hand came down on hers. "Uh, uh. I want to look at the pretty woman who's been hiding behind those glasses for years. I take it these," he held up her glasses, "are part of your camouflage?" She blushed and lowered her eyes. "Alice, don't tell me you've been acting out Grimm's fairytale about the ugly duckling turning into the beautiful swan?" He was teasing her, but at the same time knew there was some truth in his comment.

Alice felt tears gathering in her eyes. How long had it been since a man had looked her way or said she was pretty? She took a sip of water before making up her mind to tell Bert why she was hiding, and from whom. She took a sip of coffee, wiped her mouth and began slowly. "I was, and still am, running from an abusive husband, who tried to kill me twice, and said he'd finish the job one day."

"Oh Alice, Alice!" The words were out of his mouth before he could stop them. "Surely your husband was being overly dramatic. No sane man would want to...." Bert stopped in mid-sentence, realizing what he had done. He'd not only disregarded his training as a counselor, but discounted her fears, after encouraging her to talk them out with him. He'd blown it. How dare he question the veracity of her knowledge! Bert groaned softly and looked over at her. Alice's face was ashen as she put her head down on one cupped hand, elbow resting on the table. He reached over and took her free hand in his. "I wouldn't blame you if you sought someone else for counseling. I've disgraced myself by questioning your ability to see things as they were. My only defense—I couldn't believe that any man could actually tell his wife he was going to kill her. I am truly, truly sorry, and if you'll give me another chance to prove I'm genuinely interested in helping you, I will be eternally grateful."

Alice could see the pain in Bert's eyes. She nodded somberly then said, "Pastor, that's one reason I've confided in no one. But eventually I told my sister Mona. She believes that even in today's society, women can be trapped in an unspeakable marriage without a way of escape. I wake up some nights shaking, when my dreams are invaded by incidents from the past. I'm in constant fear that one of George's investigators will find me and force me to return to him. He will either kill me or have me committed. He swore that if I ever left him or tried to divorce him, he would declare me incompetent, losing my mind, a threat to my safety, as well as to his. Looking at pictures of me before I met him and the way I looked when I ran, would be used to concur that I was going crazy. George has powerful doctors of psychiatry that would willing concur with anything he has to say. I had changed dramatically. My clothes hung on me. He discouraged me from going to the salon so my hair was dull and straggly. He forbade visits to the spa; said he didn't want me flaunting my body to anyone but him. I no longer kept in touch with my friends; didn't want them talking about my appearance. Pastor, pride played such a part in the scenario; George knew it, and used it."

"So his name is George. What's his surname? What does he do for a living?"

"George Darlington; he's a stockbroker."

"Ah. So he has a good income?" She nodded. "How did you meet him?"

"I was the office manager of a stockbroker firm; George often consulted Baxter, head of our firm. I knew him by sight but never had a conversation with him in the office. I didn't know too much about him till we met at a stockbrokers' convention in New York. We bumped into each other;

neither of us had come with a partner, so we chatted and ate together... glad to have someone to interact with. Makes for a better evening." Bert nodded, knowing the feeling now that Jenny was gone.

"Before the night was over he asked for my cell number; said he'd call me. He did a couple of days later. I wasn't dating anyone at the time, and George acted very interested in hanging around. I was thrilled. I was in my forties, feeling the emptiness and loneliness many women experience who've sacrificed love, marriage, and children for a career. I had made it to the top, was financially secure. The brick home I'd inherited from my parents was in a good neighborhood. But my evenings were getting longer and lonelier. After four months of dining out and going to the theater, he asked me to marry him. I was caught off guard; it was sooner than I'd expected. But, I said yes. The next night he produced a gorgeous diamond solitaire and put it on my ring finger. I could hardly wait to get to work to show it off to my colleagues, to see them drool with envy!"

She stopped talking, took a sip of water and shook her head. "I'm ashamed when I think of the gloating I did over my good fortune. I bragged and boasted about George: his looks, his financial security, etc., etc. I laid it on thick. All that boasting and gloating came back to haunt me when I had to hide from them, lest they saw my misery."

Bert nodded. "How often we find pleasure in boasting over something, knowing our boasting is hurting someone else. It's a common flaw in us all, Alice."

Alice looked at Bert earnestly. "At that time, I was the happiest woman on the planet. I had everything a woman could ask for. A career, a lovely home, and now a man with whom I could share the rest of my life."

"What went wrong with this perfect picture, Alice?" Bert, sipping cold coffee, grimaced.

She moved her glass around in a circle before looking over at him. "We started talking wedding dates. Church affiliation had never been a part of our conversations. I had been a member of First Presbyterian for years; didn't attend as often as I should have...but I considered myself a nominal Christian. When I asked him what church he wanted to get married in, he said without any apology, 'No church. I gave church up long ago. I want to elope, skip all the falderals connected with a church wedding. We're middle age adults, don't need to hear "Here Comes the Bride." We can get some minister to say the words, sign the license, and make it legal.'"

Bert listened in silence but was groaning within. How could Alice have submitted to his wishes; trashed all her dreams of walking down the aisle in her glorious bridal gown to meet her groom?

It took courage for her to tell Bert what came next. "You didn't know George. When I bucked at his suggestion of eloping, said I wanted a church wedding, do you know what he said?" Bert shook his head, dreading what was coming next.

"'Have your wedding, Alice. And when the groom doesn't show up at the altar, explain the reason to all your guests.'"

Bert spluttered after taking a sip of water. "He said he'd be a no-show... you'd be jilted?" Alice nodded.

Bert was shaking his head in disbelief. A passing waitress filled his cup and topped Alice's. "That's when you should have given him back his ring, Alice." Against his better judgment he'd spoken.

She nodded. "I knew that by then Bert, but my ego and overindulged pride were things I couldn't ignore. What my friends would say if I called off the wedding, I would never be able to live down. I e-mailed friends closest to me, enthusing over the elopement deal. It sounded so, so romantic. George couldn't wait, wanted me now, not months from now. It was a piece of garbage, and my heart was breaking at the thought of giving up my dream wedding. George knew I would go along with him... because he knew how much my pride was involved. I played the fool, Bert, and reaped a miserable, miserable harvest. We flew to Las Vegas Friday afternoon and got married in a sleazy wedding chapel by a grizzly old man who mumbled the words. The background music came from some CD and two paid witnesses completed the package deal. It was humiliating and disgusting. A taxi took us to the airport and we were back in New York. I spent my honeymoon in the house I inherited from Mom and Dad. George had moved some of his things in before we left town."

Bert didn't open his mouth for fear of expressing his disgust in words unbecoming to his profession. He shook his head at her naiveté. Alice looked at him shamefacedly. "I was asking for it, wasn't I, Bert, when I went along with elopement?" Bert just shrugged.

Alice picked up her coffee cup, a prelude to deciding how much to tell about her wedding night. She could not tell him what George had done and made her do; it was too humiliating...too degrading. There had been no love making; George completely invaded her body with a ferocity that both sickened and revolted her. When she cried because of inflicted pain, George laughed; her pain seemed to heighten his erotic pleasure.

When he fell asleep from physical exhaustion, she crept out of bed. She stood under the hot shower, water mixing with unstoppable tears coursing down her cheeks. Nausea hit her. She knelt at the toilet and retched until her stomach ached. Taking a nightgown and a terry robe hanging behind the bathroom door, she crept downstairs and lay curled up on the couch in the family room, wrapped in a caftan.

George shook her awake the next morning. "Hey, why are you down here? Too much partying last night, Allison?" He grinned sardonically. "You'll get used to it through time." He patted her shoulder and went toward the kitchen.

She heard him fiddling with the coffee machine, and moaned. "Oh God...what am I going to do? What kind of a monster have I married?"

Their waitress interrupted her memories like a visiting angel. "What about dessert?"

Bert looked over at Alice, who looked a bit dazed and uncertain. "Yeah, I think we could use something to sweeten our palates. What have you got to offer?" The waitress recited the pies, cakes, puddings, and ice creams available.

"What about it Alice?"

She grinned and nodded. "I'll have a vanilla sundae with caramel topping, please," she smiled over at Bert.

"How about bringing me a slice of carrot cake...that'll do it. And, maybe some fresh coffee?" He held up their cups. The waitress nodded, took the empty cups and left.

"Alice, I don't want to hear anything you're uncomfortable talking about. I just need to have an idea what he's capable of pulling off. I know you're concerned about investigators, so we want to strategize our movement for any situation. Rest assured, Alice, you're not going through this alone. The church and I will be there for you." He grinned sheepishly at her.

Alice nodded and let out a sigh of relief. "Thanks Bert. I lived in fear of upsetting George; I watched what I did and what I said, his temper in mind. My office became my sanctuary. I began leaving for work early, eating breakfast in a restaurant before getting to the office. On the way home, I'd buy our dinner from a nice deli. On one particular night George saw me dishing out Chinese from take away cartons. He threw the empty carton at me and shouted, 'I'm sick of eating deli food. I want home cooked meals. Married women are supposed to cook meals that please their husbands. Don't see you doing that. You're working too much. I want you to quit your job; you have a job here you're neglecting. I don't need what you earn. So give Baxter your notice in the morning.'"

"I was furious. No way was he going to take away the job I'd sacrificed everything for. My job was the only tangible thing I had left of my self-esteem. I screamed that it would never happen...I'd never quit my job. While I was still talking, he took his hand and slapped my face so hard that I fell backward onto the floor. He didn't try to help me up, or say he was sorry. But through gritted teeth he told me, 'You'll do as I say or I'll do it for you and go talk to him myself. The firm's working you too hard... it's interfering with our marital happiness. Give them notice, and begin packing up your office.'"

"I was traumatized; my face burned, but the horror of George making a scene at my office was more than I could handle. My horrible marriage would be on display if he had his way. Again the thought of my colleagues surfaced. I had no option; George did not make idle threats. I picked myself up, went to our bedroom and locked the door. From that night on he slept in the guest room. When the sexual urge came, he was in my bed, mauling me...not making love. It was during these visits that he pressed those vulnerable places in the neck that can render one unconscious. I was unconscious for only a few moments, but heard him say, 'One night you won't wake up.'"

Bert shook his head, his face ashen. "Oh Alice, Alice...it's a miracle you survived. Under such tyranny you had no option but to give up your job...you were boxed in." She nodded.

"How long had you been married when you ran?"

"Not quite two years. But the thought of running never left me. I was planning escape all the time. How and when was the conundrum. George is a sadist, knew how to manipulate my mind. Often he'd warn that if I ran, he'd have me committed. Would show authorities how I once looked and how I now looked. I'd lost weight, my hair was a mess, my skin was sallow. He would have used my present appearance to justify what he said about me losing my mind. Even having to quit my job at his demand would look like I was unable to cope with the outside world. I stayed home, had no friends—George had made a scene when I had friends over. I was ashamed of the way I looked. I went out only to grocery shop. I cared little for mall shopping. What was the use? I was going nowhere."

"You had a car?"

"Oh yes...the one I had before I met him. Why didn't I just gas up and keep on going? Sounds easy, but knowing George I knew he'd find me. Put that together with the fact that I had plenty of money in my checking account. George made sure of that; plus I had access to $50,000 in our joint savings account. Who would believe my story that I was running away from a monster, with all that money at my disposal? I was in a bind, and I knew it."

Bert nodded. "Yeah, I can see how his devious mind worked. He gave you everything to make you happy, but you were losing it...the mind playing tricks. Such a powerful man, and with others ready to do his bidding, you could have been railroaded into some institution. George would do his bit of weeping, wailing, maybe even gnashing his teeth, but he'd have completely destroyed you. Bastard!" Bert gritted his teeth at the cruelty involved. "But more than that, it sounds to me that he was demon possessed. We know little about demon possession, only that Satan lends himself to anyone wanting the power he offers. I can't judge, that's God's office, but that guy needs help before he meets his Maker. Men like George open themselves up to demon possession, when they have a diabolical hatred for something or someone.

"Could be he had a quirk about successful women; they were a threat to his maleness. As a successful woman you were the epitome of everything he despised, so he set out to reduce you to the status of subservience. His power increased as your self-esteem decreased."

Alice looked at him wide-eyed. "You know Bert, that makes more sense than anything I've been able to come up with, as to the reason he wanted to destroy me. The last thing of importance he demanded was my job; then he would have killed me...mission accomplished."

"So how did you finally get up the courage to leave the jerk? How did you get away without detection?"

The waitress appeared with their desserts. "Time out Alice to enjoy the pleasures of calories that will add a bit to our waists in the morning." She grinned and put a spoon of ice cream to her mouth. Bert took a bite of cake. "Mmmm, good."

Alice smiled, glad to finally be able to confide in someone. She savored the ice cream until Bert raised his eyebrows signaling he was waiting to hear about her escape. "No one knew the truth about my situation. Well, my sister Mona did, but she lived in upstate New York. Mona begged me to come to her place; but knowing George, it would be the first place he'd look. I started gathering important documents, you know, the deed to my house—still in my maiden name; life insurance policy, list of stocks and bonds, checking account number...everything of value I'd accumulated over the years. I also wrote out the details of every perverted act inflicted on me by George, plus his threats to kill me. On one of my grocery trips, I stopped at a notary, dated my statements, signed it in front of her; two of her office employees witnessed my signature.

"I mailed everything to Mona via registered mail. I warned Mona that when I ran, I would be incommunicado from everyone. I would get in touch with her but she would not be able to contact me, for both our protection. I stored my expensive jewelry in a safe deposit box in another bank under my mother's maiden name; kept a few items out that I might need to sell if I ran out of money. I hid my jewelry case inside an overnight bag, added underwear and a change of clothes, put the overnight bag under my bed and waited for the opportune moment to arrive. Every time I went grocery shopping, I filled up my gas tank so it would always be ready if I used the car for my escape. The plans kept me sane and alert."

Alice looked over at Bert. His eyes told her he was sympathizing with her situation and believing her narrative. She felt safe and grateful that at last she could talk about her ordeal with someone who listened and believed her.

"George's nightly ritual was predictable. He would eat dinner, go to his office, or to the family room, watch television then go to bed. We seldom talked; never went out together to a restaurant or a movie. I busied myself in the kitchen and stayed out of his orbit. Some nights I would go to the basement and do a load of laundry, just to stay away from him. The night before I ran, I went to the basement to do some laundry. When I finished the washing and drying cycles I went up the stairs. I couldn't believe it—he had locked the basement door. I shouted and began beating on the door, demanding he unlock it. He shouted back that I was where I belonged...with the rest of the vermin. This humiliation was greater than the discomfort. My mother had made a little sitting room in the basement, with an old couch and a stuffed chair. George had never gone down to the basement. I really got scared; I knew his erratic behavior was escalating. I feared for my life and knew I had to get away regardless of the risk involved.

"I spent the night planning. George unlocked the door the next morning; yelled down that he'd left a list of things for me to pick up for him. He told me not to bother fixing dinner, he had a meeting in Boston and would be late coming home. By then George was so sure I was cowed enough, too traumatized to leave him, he didn't bother warning me against trying 'any funny stuff' as he called it."

Bert finished the last of his carrot cake and chased crumbs around the plate with his finger. He was incensed that he had waited all this time to find out what had troubled Alice for years. An urge to go to her, put his arms around her, was so strong he had to fight against it. Instead, he asked diplomatically, "So what happened after he left?"

"Bert, my feet grew wings. I listened till I heard the front door close, then I came bounding up the basement stairs. I watched till he backed out of the garage and held my breath as he went down the driveway and into the street. Waited a few minutes, just in case he was playing a game with me, then I bolted up the stairs, pulled my overnight bag from under the bed, threw the rest of what I needed into it, grabbed my purse and keys, and ran to my car. I don't remember if I even locked the front door. I was on my way in less than 20 minutes. I'd rehearsed it in my mind for so long—I was on auto pilot. I shook so hard I had to watch my driving... but I was free...and I intended to stay free.

"My first stop was the bank. I went to the ATM and drew out everything in my checking account except one dollar: $1,854.00. The bank wasn't open yet, so I ate breakfast at a McDonald's across the street. I took time to put some makeup on, comb my hair, before entering the bank. At 9 a.m. I walked in and asked to speak to the bank manager. I was no stranger to him; we were good customers. I told him George wanted $25,000 from our savings account, that he wanted cash for a special deal he was involved in. The bank manager had no reason to doubt anything I said. In 15 minutes I was in my car, clutching all that money and trying to look like everything was fine. I locked the car doors, and took out enough cash for the plans I had in mind. I put cash in a secret pocket in my shoulder bag, some in my wallet. My ID and credit cards, I put in my overnight bag, along with the rest of the cash.

"Next stop was the hairdresser. I had my hair cut in a punk style, dyed an ugly brown covering the blonde. The beautician tried to discourage my choice of hair coloring but I said it was for a bit part I had in a play. She shrugged and suggested I buy a wig. But she complied. I made my way to a Goodwill store; bought a pair of jeans; two sweat shirts; an orange nylon jacket sporting a baseball logo; a pair of oxfords; and a canvas suitcase on wheels. I found out it squeaked when I pulled it. At the checkout counter I found these glasses," she held up the horned rims. She looked at his face, and laughed at his expression. "To add to the ridiculous outfit, I bought a baseball hat, turned it backwards and my disguise was complete. My whole getup cost me $18.50. I changed into my new clothes in their dressing room; put my own things including my overnight bag, in the suitcase, and walked out of the store. My new hairdo would throw any investigator off track, but in my new wardrobe, they'd never recognize me."

She leaned against the back of the booth and began to laugh until tears ran down her cheeks. Bert was flummoxed by the paroxysm of laughter, then the tears. "What...what hit your funny bone?"

She wiped her eyes with a paper napkin, grinned at Bert and answered, "When I think of what I looked like, wearing that Goodwill outfit, I'm amazed I had the audacity to do it. But I was desperate and desperation gives you courage, let me tell you. Here I am, sophisticated Allison Darlington who wore only designer outfits, walking down a New York City street in grubby clothes, wearing a baseball cap backwards with a punk hairdo peeking out, pulling a squeaky-wheeled beat up suitcase...and feeling safe in that ghastly getup. Instead of being mortified at my descent into the ridiculous, I was proud that I had the temerity to pull it off. The ugly glasses that covered my face gave me additional courage."

He looked at her smiling face, sans the specs, and thought, Allison Darlington must have been one beautiful woman.

"What did you do next, Alice?"

"From there I went to a Dollar Tree, bought a pair of scissors and a sturdy plastic envelope with a zipper, and a plastic belt. In my car I slit two lines in the plastic envelope, slipped the nylon belt through them to make a pouch, and in it I put the balance of my money. I put the belt around my waist with the pouch resting on my stomach. It looked like I had a paunch, exactly the effect I wanted. I put the sweatshirt over the pouch and was ready to go." She smiled over at him whimsically and he found his heart flipping over.

"Your story would make a great movie," he said somberly. "When did you finally get out of New York City?"

She leaned back on the bench. "When I planned my escape, knowing George, I figured I had to be devious. So, my route was as circuitous and confusing as I could make it. I drove my car to the airport's long-term parking, got a taxi outside the terminal, and had the driver take me to the train station. When he was out of sight, I made my way to the Greyhound bus terminal. I boarded the bus leaving for Florida after buying a one-way ticket south. The trip seemed endless and boring, but as long as I was in the bus, I felt safe from George. The monotony was relieved by intermittent stops for coffee and lavatory breaks. I watched passengers enter and leave at various stops, always on the lookout for anyone looking suspicious. Sleep was not an option; I had to be alert at all times.

"As the bus rolled along, I had plenty of time to peruse the travel guide, searching for some inspiration about where to hide. When we hit South Carolina, I began searching the roster for city names. Bert, the name Safe Haven fairly leaped out at me; the feeling was so strong. The bus drove slowly through Safe Haven, and I made a quick decision. I disembarked, and walked back in the direction of a motel sign I'd seen. I didn't tell the driver I was leaving...I didn't want to call attention to myself. I arrived at a decent looking motel and asked for a room. I could pay cash, but couldn't produce a credit card. I explained my wallet had been stolen with all my credentials in it. The manager agreed to let me stay one night. Eventually

I had to get fake IDs and a limited credit card. I eventually found a cheap one-room rental that cost less than the motel. I bought a decent little Ford Escort for $500, secured a job at the church, and the rest is history."

Bert was quiet for a moment as he thought about how difficult it must have been to leave everything and everyone she knew and become a different person. He was amazed at her ability to change personas and maintain her new character with ease. But, as she pointed out...she was desperate. He was reluctant to leave the restaurant; he was concerned for her now that he knew her situation.

It was Alice who got him focusing on other matters. "Pastor, do you mind if I make a suggestion about tomorrow night's meeting?"

"No, of course not."

"Plan arriving at the meeting at least 15 minutes late."

Bert, always punctual, looked at her skeptically.

She ignored his raised eyebrows, explaining, "This will give you an edge. Instead of waiting for them, they'll be waiting for you. The men will wonder if you've changed your mind about meeting with them. They'll be concerned."

Bert grinned genially. "Clever, clever. You give that advice to CEOs you worked with?"

Alice laughed and once again he saw the woman behind the façade. "Of course. The man who waits is the one who gets anxious."

"Well, I need all the edges I can get. I've an idea this is just the first of many tete-a-tetes between me and our various boards."

"What do you mean, Bert?"

"Traditional churches like ours are targeted for change. In post-modern Christian circles, churches that still hold on to traditions are viewed as dinosaurs...out of step with the 21st century millennial culture. They think that as pastors we should put social issues of this generation as first priority in our sermons. The gospel of salvation is of secondary or even of tertiary importance. Youth must be served; they're the future church. Death is far off; the nasty here and now is what they want addressed. Preaching about man's responsibility to God's laws...too crass, homophobic, politically incorrect." Bert took a last sip of water, shrugged his shoulders and confessed, "I can't change my message, Alice. Jesus faulted the church at

Ephesus for leaving off preaching the gospel of salvation. He warned them to return to the reason the church existed, or they would lose their church.

"Alice, churches are preaching messages people want to hear, not what God wants them to hear. But men still die; young and old alike, and all will stand before their Maker. It's the minister's duty to get his flock ready to meet God. When I accepted the call to preach, it was to seek and to save the lost. Till then I'll keep trying to bring in the sheaves."

They parted at their cars. "Goodnight Alice, see you in the morning."

"Goodnight, Pastor."

Before sleep finally claimed him that night, Bert's last thought was of Alice.

CHAPTER THREE

The first thing to enter Bert's mind the next morning was Alice. He headed into the office, settled into his chair, and groaned, wondering how he'd act with his emotions playing havoc with his gut, when she was suddenly at the door.

The knock was timid. "Come in."

Alice put the coffee tray and letters on his desk. Bert, head down, barely nodded. She felt his reserve and turned to leave. Alice had dreaded this meeting, concerned that she had divulged too much of her past to him at the restaurant. Her hand was on the doorknob when Bert said quietly, "Alice, don't go. Grab a cup of coffee...we need to talk some more." His gentle voice brought tears to her eyes.

Seated across from him, she sipped at the coffee. Bert laid his glasses on the desk, rubbed his bleary eyes, and looked her way. He grinned sheepishly. "Humor me...take off those glasses, let me look at the real you while we talk." She blushed, relaxed, and complied. The ugly glasses were removed.

"Thanks. I didn't get much sleep last night worrying about your situation. Years ago, when I sensed you were afraid of something, I should have inquired then. Other things got in the way; Jenny got sick...." He trailed off.

"I know it's a day late and a dollar short, but Alice, you're family; you're no longer fighting this alone. If any goon comes sniffing around, we're going to show him what southern un-hospitality looks like.

"So what I need is your permission to talk to my friend Glen Roberts in the D.A.'s office; be apprised of extradition laws in South Carolina in case your husband tries to take you back to New York on the pretext that you're mentally unbalanced. I want to know what protective measures are available under such circumstances." He saw her shiver and remarked, "Alice if you can, relax in the knowledge that you're not alone anymore. I'm here for you. This too shall pass; nothing remains the same, and God will put closure to your ordeal in His own way and in His own time."

Bert looked at Alice standing by the door and saw tears running down her cheeks. He rose and went to her, put his arms around her and held her protectively. She leaned into his chest momentarily, then withdrew. They were embarrassed at the emotion the brief encounter had aroused. Alice, without looking at him, left the office. Bert knew he was in love with her; the perversity of the situation grabbed him. She was a married woman, and should she divorce George, his dedication to biblical principles were deeply rooted. Many of his peers had continued preaching after a divorce and remarriage, but Bert believed there was no true happiness in ignoring God's standards. He sat down clumsily behind his desk and thought of the irony of the situation. After Jenny's death, he had banked his emotions as one banked a fire, with ashes and cinders. That he should find dead embers coming to life flummoxed him completely. That the instinct to mate still existed floored, and embarrassed him. But, he had fallen in love with Alice, in spite of her appearance. He sighed contemplatively. "God help me. I need help—now!"

Some of the deacons came on time, some sauntered in later, augmenting their place in the pecking order. Gregory Hunt, the youngest and newest deacon, juxtaposed his position in the church with his position as bank manager of Community National Bank. Gregory expected, and usually was accorded, special attention when he spoke—whether what he said was of any real consequence or not. When Alice, John Folk, and Scott Martin entered the office, deacon eyebrows rose. Why were they included in a deacons' meeting?

"Where's the pastor?" one man asked, looking over at Alice, who wisely kept her eyes on her steno pad.

"Probably needs a new watch," another deacon quipped. Laughter. Tension was mounting when the Rev. Robert Davenport made an unhurried entrance, nodded to the group, settled behind his desk, and made no reference to his lateness.

Bert spoke. "Well, let's get this meeting started. Gregory, please ask the Lord's blessing on our meeting, that it will be profitable."

Hunt was caught completely off guard. He struggled to exorcise the nasty words from his mind in reference to the preacher, and replace them with spiritual ones. He cleared his throat, and invoked God's blessing on the gathering, wrapping up with, "...and Lord, we look to You for wisdom and guidance for the growth of our church in this new millennium. In Christ's name we pray, Amen."

"Thanks Gregory. Now Bob, let's begin with you. Bring us up to date concerning this evangelist. Where he comes from, churches he's pastored, seminary background, doctrinal belief, and the importance of his message to our congregation. Give us a rundown on the guy...sorry, the evangelist."

With the ball passed to him, Bob Billingsly suddenly felt inadequate to talk about the personal side of the speaker the deacons had already invited without informing Davenport of their action. "Well," he began, clearing his throat. "To tell the truth I don't know as much about Dr. Faulkner as I should. I was so carried away with his message about the condition of mainline churches, that I failed to ask personal questions about his background. There were so many people crowding around him—I didn't have a chance to talk to him much. But, from what I gathered, he started out as a pastor in a northern church; taught church history at a seminary in the Midwest; got some kind of grant from some corporation to do a survey on why mainline churches in America are losing members and closing doors. With the grant, he's traveled the country, taken polls, gathered data, and published his findings. His information has been well-received by mainline churches and he is in demand as a speaker. He is knowledgeable and is a dynamic speaker. I felt our church could really profit by hearing his message."

"Amen to that," commented an enthusiast.

"One of the best," echoed Hunt.

Bert listened without comment, knowing where consensus lay. Dr. Faulkner would speak to the church, regardless of Pastor Davenport's approval or disapproval. He tried not to be prejudicial before meeting the man. Bert picked up the ball. "Does the reverend..."

"He has an earned doctorate," corrected Gregory Hunt insolently.

"Well," continued Bert unfazed, "we'll certainly see that the good doctor is given due respect. So, Bob, is the doctor a married man? Does he have a family?"

Bob squirmed in his seat. "I didn't ask, Bert. I will when I talk to him after our meeting."

"Fine. What seminary did he graduate from? What doctrine does he espouse?"

Bob sighed heavily. "Gee, Bert, I can see I didn't do my homework on the guy, erg, on the doctor. But I'll find out when I talk with him. OK?"

Bert felt sorry for Bob, and although he had more questions to put to him, decided he'd gain nothing but hostility from the other deacons if he pursued any further in his quest for knowledge about the Dr. Faulkner.

But Gregory Hunt, bent on pontificating, had to make a point. "What difference does it make if Faulkner's a married man with 10 kids, or a eunuch with none? It's the message we're interested in, not his sex life, or where he went to seminary." Laughter.

"Touché," Bert said amicably. "But let me ask you a question, Gregory. If a man came into your bank for a loan of say, $10,000 and you'd never met him before, didn't know if he had any assets, would you be apt to lend him money on the strength of his impressive rhetoric?" Hunt's face turned scarlet. He knew the preacher was right—background did matter.

"In the case of our guest speaker," Bert continued, "isn't it prudent that your pastor knows what doctrine the speaker espouses, how he feels about the Bible, the doctrine we ascribe to in our church? I would have to say it is of utmost importance that we find out everything we can about any speaker that stands behind the pulpit of this church."

There was a shuffling of feet, a clearing of throats. Bert had made his point, no use lingering. He continued addressing Bob. "What kind of advertising did the board come up with for the coming meeting?"

"Advertising?" asked Bob in a confused tone. "Wouldn't making announcements from the pulpit Sundays and Wednesday nights before the meeting do?"

"Well sure, if all you want to reach is our own congregation. Yeah, we could do that."

"What did you have in mind, preacher?" Alan Baxter inquired.

"Usually when we have guest speakers, we print flyers announcing the meeting, info about the speaker, his subject matter...you know, pertinent info."

"Yeah," said another deacon. "I think we do need to advertise. Dr. Faulkner might encourage new people to come to our church after hearing him."

Nods and amens came from the group. "Yeah," said Bob. "Let's get flyers into neighborhoods."

Bert almost choked on the next item he was about to bring up. "Bob when you talk with Dr. Faulkner and get that information, give it to Alice before the end of the week. She'll see that flyers are printed and ready for delivery."

Bob made a note on a scrap of paper, and nodded.

Pastor nodded toward the young man sitting with Folk and Alice. "You all know Scott Martin, he's our youth director. Scott, do you think you can round up some volunteers to pass out flyers?"

"Well, I'll put it to the kids at our regular Saturday night get-together, and let you know."

"How many flyers you figuring on distributing, Bob?" asked Scott.

Bert appreciated the way Scott directed the question to Bob, who in turn looked startled to have the ball he thought he'd gotten rid of back in his lap. He struggled to fend off the missile. "How many did your kids pass out last time, Scott?"

"We had 400 flyers; passed out 200 one Saturday morning, last bunch the following Saturday. We started in neighborhoods farthest from the church, finished in neighborhoods nearest the church."

"Let's go with that same number this time," proffered Bob, content to pass the ball to Scott.

"Sounds good," said Scott. "Now we'll have to have chaperones for the kids," he amended. Bert could have kissed him.

"Chaperones!" bellowed Gregory Hunt. "We're not asking you to get three- and four-year-old kids climbing porches with flyers clutched in their hands for pity sake. Pre-teens and teens don't need chaperons."

Gregory Hunt's incredulous remark had Bert biting his tongue to keep from laughing. He waited for Martin's retort.

Martin, a free spirit who wasn't impressed or cowed by Gregory's social status, countered dryly. "Mr. Hunt," he said with panache. "We don't let children go house to house without supervision these days, it isn't safe. A car and driver will take two or three kids to a designated street. While the kids work both sides of the street the driver follows slowly down the road keeping an eye on the kids. If we have fourteen kids, we'll need seven cars and drivers. Things have changed, Mr. Hunt. Even Halloween trick-or-treaters have moms or dads trailing along, keeping an eye out for trouble.

"And," Scott continued, "I suggest that when the kids have finished running up and down stairs, you take them out for a meal. Maybe Chick-fil-A or wherever; a thank you treat for a job well done." He nodded to Bert, and resumed his seat.

Gregory Hunt was nursing a slow burn of anger and humiliation. He put these unforeseen roadblocks at the feet of Robert Davenport. The board was discovering that proposing an idea was much simpler than implementing it.

Bert cleared his throat, got their attention and inquired, "Did you discuss an honorarium, Bob? If so, how much? This we DO need to know specifically."

Feet shuffled, throats cleared, coughing ensued.

Bob looked pained, searching his notes to delay giving an answer that he knew would not be received well, and said meekly, "We said something like a $1500 honorarium."

Bert heard a gasp. Didn't have to look, knew it came from John Folk the church treasurer. He kept his silence till the shock wave subsided, then he turned to John.

"How's the budget fixed for honorariums, John?"

"Right now, the only honorarium we're involved with is trying to honor our commitment to getting a new roof for the children's department. Every time it rains, the kids get wet. We're trying to collect enough for repairs or for a new roof. So to answer your question, we've got zilch in any fund outside the one for the roof. You'd sooner get 1500 bucks out of a turnip than out of our treasury." John Folk was shaking his head in disbelief; muttering sotto voce, "1500 bucks!"

Bert turned to Bob, who was sweating and tugging at his shirt collar. "Any suggestions on raising the money, Bob?" Bert asked kindly. He hated to see this good guy take all the heat. But, he'd put his foot in his mouth willingly, now it was up to him to either chew it or spit it out. Bert waited, then asked, "If not, may I make a suggestion?"

Bob looked up like a man seeking that proverbial cup of cold water. "Yeah, sure Bert, anything."

"When you call Dr. Faulkner why not lay the facts concerning the penurious condition of our treasury before him? Say we could pony up maybe $500. But no more. Could be he'll be amenable to that; if not, he's made the decision not to come."

Bob brightened. "Yeah, I think that's a great idea Pastor, thanks." Bob was by now hoping Faulkner would say no dice, and Bob would be off all the encumbering hooks. He was sick of this business. Why had he let Hunt and a couple of the others talk him into pulling this stunt on the pastor, just to show Bert that they had power?

"Hate to ask this, Bob," continued Bert.

A weary Bob looked up. What next?

"The speaker's accommodations for Saturday night? Are we responsible? What about Sunday night? Ditto?"

Bob relaxed. "His accommodations for both nights are taken care of. Thank God for small blessings," he added. And Bert did laugh.

"Should the church have a dinner in Dr. Faulkner's honor?" Davenport wanted to appear more solicitous now that he'd given them an idea of what it took to coalesce any kind of a meeting. No one was forthcoming with an idea. Their energies were spent. They just wanted to get home and gripe to their wives how the preacher snookered them with questions, instead of them snookering him with a speaker from nowhere.

"Why not just take the guy out?" said a disgruntled Gregory Hunt. He knew the preacher had been right to ask the questions but was furious that they hadn't had the foresight to anticipate them. As active deacons, their preparation for the meeting had been meager; their performance, dismal. Hunt carried a grudge against Bert. This exposure of their ignorance only heightened the angst he felt for the pastor.

"Church pay for the dinner?" asked John Folk, keeper of the Lord's cash.

"Nah," said Hunt disgustedly. I'll pay for HIS meal, myself."

"Let's wrap up then. Don't forget to give Alice all pertinent info for the flyers. Pete, why don't you close in prayer?"

Pete Henderson complied; his prayer was brief. He thanked God for everyday mercies, and finished with, "And God, give us the wisdom we need to fill the office of deacon. In Jesus name we pray, Amen."

The meeting broke up with a whimper rather than a harangue, each deacon cosseting his own thoughts, exiting quietly and as quickly as decency allowed. Gregory Hunt lingered, hoping for a chance at the pastor, to chew him out for making them look like a bunch of incompetent imbeciles. Bob was still talking to Davenport. Frustrated, Gregory left in a huff, determined to spew his bile over Bert at the first opportunity.

They walked to their cars companionably. "Pastor, I want to apologize again for creating this mess. I should've kept my own counsel rather than listen to the others. I knew we were wrong by not asking your permission before inviting Faulkner. But once the ball was kicked, I had to run with it."

Reaching his car, Bert put out his hand. "Bob, don't be too hard on yourself. It was a lesson you'll not forget; we all learn from mistakes. But get all the info you can on our speaker. God holds me accountable for words uttered from my pulpit, into the ears of my congregation."

"Count on it, Pastor. I'll follow up on that right away. Goodnight."

CHAPTER FOUR

The answering machine was chattering away delivering a message when Alice entered her little abode. "Mona," she screamed, grabbing the phone in desperation. "You know better than to dial me direct, now I'll have to find another place to stay. What on earth made you..." she was crying hysterically.

"Allie, Allie, it's okay honey...it's okay. You don't have to hide anymore, he's gone...can't hurt you anymore."

"Gone...gone? Who's gone? What are you talking about, Mona?" Trembling with fear and apprehension, Alice had trouble understanding Mona's reply.

"Allison, settle down and listen to me. I'd rather tell you face to face, but I don't know where you are, haven't seen you in seven years. But honey," Mona's voice softened, "George is dead." Silence at both ends of the line. Mona continued. "He was killed early this morning when he hit a cement construction barrier. Apparently he was trying to avoid hitting a semi-truck, lost control of his car. Police say he must have been going 90 miles an hour when he hit the barrier. According to the police, George's upper body went through the windshield...his head was almost decapitated; he wasn't wearing a seatbelt. He died before police arrived."

Alice sat down on a kitchen chair too shocked to speak, her eyes staring at nothing. Mona added more details but they were lost on Alice. Her mind was blank, her emotions frozen. The word "FREE" darted in and out of her mind, but found no lodging place.

Mona rattled on. "Mr. Albert Thornton, George's attorney, tracked me down a little while ago. Said he had a time finding me. It was he who gave me the news about George. He's anxious to meet you; wants you to come to New York as soon as possible to sign papers. You're the widow and there are papers to be signed related to George's affairs."

Alice's mind went from a state of incredulity, to one of reason when Mona told her that she was needed in New York to sign papers belonging to George. Were he alive, Alice signing anything that belonged to him was unthinkable. So, she mused silently, George, the flaunter of evil, the despiser of good, hadn't been in control of how and when and where he should die. God made those arrangements for George, without any advance notice.

Mona broke through Alice's morbid reverie. "Allie...say something, sweetie. I know it's a lot to take in. But I've got to get back to Thornton and let him know I've contacted you about George's death. When can he expect you in his office? I've got to call him." With her duty discharged, weariness engulfed her and Mona began to cry. Alice heard her and made an effort to comfort her distraught sister.

"I'm sorry Mona. I'm having a time sorting things out, but tell the attorney I've things to tend to here; I need to check with my boss, and get myself back in some kind of shape or you'll never recognize me. I'll plan to meet with him next Tuesday morning, say around 11 a.m. I'll leave here for New York sometime Friday afternoon. Mona, this is something I don't want to wake up and find it's all a dream. It's been so long since we spoke without fear of discovery, and...." Alice began sobbing along with Mona over the land line.

"It's going to be okay Allie...we'll get you back to where you once were. I'll take care of Mr. Thornton. I can't wait to see you; love you Allie." They disconnected.

Alice sat staring into space like someone returning from a long flight dealing with jet lag: legs rubbery, head dull. Whatever George had left, bills or whatever, didn't matter. He had given her the best gift of all, her FREEDOM. She'd deal with his earthly detritus gladly. The kitchen clock said it was 7:20.

Her mind went to Bert. He would still be at the office; he had a counseling session with a couple at 8 p.m. She put timidity aside and dialed him. When Bert picked up on the second ring, he was surprised to hear her voice. "Alice, you seldom call after work. Something up?" he asked, imagining the worst.

"Pastor." Long silence ensued.

"Alice?" Bert grew anxious. "What's up?"

She choked back tears and in a strangled voice said, "My sister Mona was on the phone when I got home." Alice's voice was cracking up with sobs. "Mona told me..." She was crying hysterically, sobbing over the line.

Bert's heart was racing. "Do you want me to come to your place?" he searched.

"No, no, Bert, I'm sorry, sorry, it's just so sudden...so awful." She stopped. Bert heard her blow her nose before returning to the phone. "Mona told me George died in a terrible car accident early this morning." She let the flood gates open and Bert heard her shaky breaths between sobs.

"I'd better come and see what I can do for you Alice...this isn't news you need to handle alone. It won't take me long to counsel my lovebirds. When I'm done here I can stop and bring Ruth Anderson with me."

"No, no. Bert I'm OK. I'm just struggling with two sets of emotions that are pulling me apart. I know I should grieve over his horrible death, and yet part of me is happy that he's gone and I'm free of him."

Bert understood her dilemma. We feel righteous if we accept blame for whatever; callous if we face the truth of the situation and lay blame where it really belongs.

"Dry your tears, Alice; rejoice in your deliverance. God, not you, took George out of this world. Don't feel like you have to weep over him; that doesn't honor God's judgment. You are not being callous by rejoicing in your freedom. Don't spoil your new lease on life by fretting over the way God delivered you. Rejoice that He heard your prayers."

"Thanks Pastor, that helps. I'll be going to New York on Friday. His attorney wants me to sign business papers of George's. And of course, I'll see to his cremation, which was his wish for his remains. He hated church services, so that's something I won't have to handle. I'll check on my house; see a realtor about handling the sale and an estate sale as well." Alice was finding comfort talking about concrete matters.

"You've no idea how long you'll be gone?" He didn't wait for a reply before blurting out, "But you are coming back, right?" Bert had difficulty breathing waiting for her answer.

"Of course, that is if my job's still there," she laughed shakily.

"You know better than that Alice. You're part of us." He wanted to say more, but now wasn't the time to go maudlin. "Anything I can do to help? What about money? And I can get you to the airport, no problem." He waited.

"No, I can't think of anything I need. I'm okay, now that I can access my checking account. George still kept money in it, I'm sure hoping I'd use some so he could track me down." She signed heavily, remembering she was free to use her own money also. "I'm going to get a late flight—I've got so much to do tomorrow to make myself presentable. My sister wouldn't recognize me in this awful hairdo and drab clothes. I won't be in the office tomorrow if that's okay. Oh yes, and the flyers are ready for Bob. He got the info to me Wednesday and I got right on them. They're near the printer. I'll call Ruthie to fill in for me."

"I'll let Bob know." Bert was at a loss for words. "Let me at least drive you to the airport," he offered again.

She demurred. "Thanks, but I'd rather drive and leave my car in the long-term parking area. That way I won't bother anyone whatever time I return home."

Bert knew that insisting wasn't in the cards. Alice was trying her wings, wanted to be in control of her comings and goings. "Sure," he agreed. "I understand. But if you get a chance, give me a ring...let me know how things are going." He felt a loss, even while she was still on the other end of the line. "Well, let's have a word of prayer for your journey, Alice."

"Sure Pastor." The tears were back in her voice.

"Dear God," Bert began, "give Alice a safe trip to New York, and strength for the ordeal she faces burying of her husband. Thank you, God, for answering our prayers even as we ask. In Jesus name we pray, Amen. Goodnight Alice."

"Goodnight Pastor."

He replaced the phone in its cradle and stood looking out his office window surveying the parking lot. It needs major overhauling, he thought morosely. The once yellow lines were dirty shadows of their former brightness. Seemed like yesterday that he and Jenny had entered the parking lot as pastor of Fair Haven Baptist Church. Small cracks then were now cavernous depressions in some places.

Jenny had pointed out with pride the stenciled sign PASTOR on the red brick building. "Wow! Rev. Davenport you have been elevated in the ecclesiastical world when you get your own parking spot."

He remembered grinning and lifting his head high in mock affectation. He thought of the visions he'd had of doing great things for the Lord at Fair Haven Baptist. How much had he really contributed here? Yes, countless souls had been won to Jesus. He'd officiated at dozens of weddings, conducted untold numbers of funerals, and dedicated a slew of babies. By the time he counted counseling and comforting the bereaved and hurting, he'd been busy in his role as shepherd.

Had the measure of his worth been laid out for him by the board of trustees who'd left an hour ago? Like Job's comfortless friends, they assured him that they had not come to criticize, but only to advise.

"Pastor," the board had intoned solemnly. "Your sermons on man's responsibility to God aren't going down well with the younger generation. Hellfire and brimstone messages are offensive to 21st century congregants. Members complain that your sermons make them feel uncomfortable. To repent and get right with God is archaic, and sin is a word stricken from society's dictionary these days. People want to feel free from boundaries... choose what they feel is right for them. They resent being badgered by principles that are no longer relevant. We can't roll back the calendar to the mores of the last century. The church must accommodate cultural changes, or close its doors."

Bert listened without rebuttal. Six to one; what were the odds they'd listen, especially if he'd quoted scripture in defense of his position? They were good men, concerned for the welfare of their church, and had come apologetically to counsel, not to criticize, but carrying with them "suggestions."

"Bert, a change in your appearance would help your image. Black and navy suits are too funereal. Get into something colorful; something with a little panache. Clothes make the man...even a preacher man." They'd laughed but the arrows had sharp points and hit the mark. Jocularity didn't erase stings. The board had metaphorically stripped him naked of self-worth, and of past achievements. There was little time to linger in the Slough of Despond with an engaged couple coming for counseling. Checking his watch, he saw that he had fifteen minutes to get ready. In his bathroom he doused his face in cold water, ran a comb through his hair, a toothbrush across his teeth, and was back behind his desk searching for a breath mint when a timid knock sounded.

"Come in," he called genially. Andy Smith, holding Sue Clark's hand, entered and grinned sheepishly at him. Love entered with them, chasing out the depression the board had left. "Rumor has it that you two want to get married, that right?" They nodded. "Sure I can't talk you out of it? It's not too late," he said trying to look serious. The couple looked amused. Bert grinned at the idiocy of his remark.

They protested. "No way! We ARE getting married."

Bert chuckled softly and got down to the business at hand. Using his preaching voice and looking very solemn, he distracted their attention from each other to listen to counsel. "Marriage," he intoned, "is ordained of God, principally for procreation of the human race. Love is the magnet that draws boy to girl and vice versus. In mating, they become one. Regardless of world conditions...love finds a way to marry, have children. Marriage provides a healthy environment for nurturing the young; giving children the needed parameters in which to grow. The core of Christianity is LOVE, for God our Creator is LOVE. Love never fails; it is the greatest gift God gave to man."

After discussing the principles and the extent of Christian love, Bert closed his Bible and opened his minister's handbook. He took a sip of water, smiled at the anxious faces before him, and began to delineate the duties of a Christian husband. "According to God's instructions, the man is the head of the house. Your loyalty, Andy, will belong to Sue, your wife..." He continued with a litany of duties ascribed to the husband. Turning to Sue he said, "Sue, you are to give due respect to Andy, for he is the head of the house, someday the father of your children."

Bert then discussed responsibilities of both partners; the difficulties they would face, financial, medical, emotional, etc. However, they would get through difficult adjustments and wearisome times with the help of the Lord. "Lean on the Lord for support, kids," was Bert's favorite admonition.

Questions followed about the ceremony: order of seating family members; bridesmaids, groomsmen; when and where to enter and stand; vows, lighting of the unity candle. Bert answered without notes; he'd performed countless weddings and answered multitudes of similar questions before. When they ran out of questions in Sue's notebook, Bert prayed for the wedding preparations they'd be involved in till the day of the wedding. After prayer, he shook Andy's hand, hugged Sue briefly and saw them out the door, hand in hand.

Bert stood looking out his window as they entered the parking lot; saw Andy open the passenger door, gather Sue in his arms and kiss her hungrily. It was a happier note to end his day with, than the demeaning board meeting that had preceded it.

Everyone loves a lover, he mused on his way home. Alice had invaded his mind while counseling the kids. He thought of what God had said to Adam: "It is not good that the man be alone." Now that Alice was no longer bound to a husband, the urge to find out how she felt about him was strong. He'd counseled widows and widowers seeking advice about a second marriage. Choosing a mate the second time around should be taken just a seriously as the first time.

CHAPTER FIVE

As Bert entered his house, the aroma of Mrs. Jackson's cooking teased his nostrils. Without taking off his jacket, he went to the kitchen to see what gastronomic feast she'd cooked for his empty stomach. He groaned with delight at the chicken casserole warming in the oven. The sideboard was laid out with butter, rolls, apple pie. He started coffee in the Bunn and retreated to the bathroom.

He filled his plate, sat down at the kitchen table, said grace, and tucked in. "Mmmm," he fairly sang with each mouthful. Emily Jackson was in demand as a daily domestic. Two days a week were all she could allot Bert, but she cooked enough those two days for him to nibble on till her next visit. It worked for them both.

While his mind took pleasure in feeding the physical, his inner man gave him indigestion with matters of the heart. "I know your feet are cold, but Bert, if you're going to ask her to consider dating you, you'd best do it before she leaves for New York. Let her know your intentions NOW!"

Bert, preferring procrastination to facing lions, shut down his nagger, poured another cup of aromatic coffee, and found himself dialing Alice's apartment. It was 9 p.m. He fidgeted while her phone rang. He was almost hoping she wasn't home when the phone was picked up.

"Bert," said Alice, reading caller I.D., "is something up?"

"Uh...uh...no, just wanted to check and see how you're doing. Wondered if there's anything I can do before you take off?"

"No, but Ruth will be in the office in the morning. She's set to fill in for me till I get back. I told her about Bob's flyers, where they are. I believe your correspondence is caught up; unless something came in after I left this afternoon?"

"Don't fret over anything here, Alice. You've got enough to contend with when you get to New York. What time is your plane leaving tomorrow?"

"I booked a late flight. I have so much to do tomorrow getting myself presentable. Mona would probably disown me or have a coronary if I didn't do something about my appearance." Alice laughed and Bert found himself grinning.

"D'you think you'd have time to eat lunch or dinner with me? I have something I'd like to ask you." He held his breath; what would she say?

"I hope to be finished around 3 p.m. and leave for the airport around 4. But I can try to meet you at 2:30, if that suits you."

"Perfect. If Charlie's is okay with you, I'll meet you there at 2:30. Right?"

"Sounds good. See you then, Pastor."

Bert spent the rest of the night wondering at the likelihood of Alice considering him husband material. He lifted his self-worth out of the dustbin where the Board had deposited it, and examined his credentials. Nothing to write home about; nothing startling about a small-town preacher in his 60s: hair thinning, shoulders drooping, midsection growing slightly each year. At present, a decent salary that could change any day. He remembered his advice to Ed Brown. "Don't borrow trouble, wait till you're hit with the pink slip." That sage advice gave him to courage to ignore his growing paunch and his tightening belt. Reaching for a second piece of pie he muttered aloud, "Tomorrow I'm swearing off all sweets; tomorrow I'm going to start exercising in the gym."

Alice was at the beauty parlor at 8:30 the next morning, and till noon, she turned herself over to the beautician, who worked diligently to rid her hair of the mud color and coax it back to an attractive auburn. Blonde tresses would come much later. Other beauticians worked on her fingernails and toenails while the hair was transformed. Her toweled hair was dried, the scissors began snipping away, till she thought she was getting a crew cut. "Not to worry," soothed the hairdresser, "you've got plenty left. You'll like what you see when I'm through."

When she finally was handed a mirror, Alice gasped at her image. But for the color of hair, she was Allison Evans, before...George. Tears welled up in her eyes. She nodded and murmured, "You've worked a miracle; you'll never know what this means to me." The beautician smiled, pleased with her work.

A facial came next, then makeup was applied. Alice left the salon at 12:15, and made for the most fashionable boutique in the mall. After trying on several outfits, she settled on a soft wool black suit with a long jacket that minimized the extra weight she'd gained over the years. A rose-colored silk blouse added the perfect finishing touch to the outfit.

Bert was sitting where he could see everyone entering the restaurant. With Alice on his mind, he paid scant attention to any other women, and was flummoxed when an elegant woman approached his booth, and proceeded to slide in across from him. She smiled.

"Alice?" Bert's mouth was dry; he felt dizzy; speech became a stranger to him.

"Been waiting long, Bert?" the vision asked.

"Alice! My word, my stars...you're beautiful." She began to laugh. It was the first time he could remember ever hearing her laugh without restraint. Her hair was stylish, coiffed with reddish highlights; her fingers manicured. She wore makeup that added to her beauty. Later, when reliving this moment, he would remember her black suit, the flattering rose blouse and the gold accessories that added additional class to the outfit. The booth took on the ambience of flowers from the perfume she wore. Alice was a knockout, a beautiful woman. He sat in awe. With his scripted speech shelved, he said over and over again, "Alice, you're simply beautiful."

It had been a long time since Alice felt such happiness. "Thanks Bert. Now what is it you wanted to ask me? Remember I've a plane to catch."

A waitress appeared, ready to take their orders. Bert looked at Alice. "I'll have a tossed salad, a slice of whole wheat toast and a cup of Earl Grey tea. Thank you."

The waitress looked at Bert. "I'll have a Reuben on rye, no onions, and coffee. Thanks."

They sat staring awkwardly, seeing each other as if for the first time. Tea and coffee helped mitigate the awkward impasse. Every once in a while, Bert looked over at her and shook his head. "Unbelievable," he commented.

Alice finally moved away from her appearance and reminded, "You said you had something to discuss with me, Pastor?"

Bert's face reddened. Alice's feminine intuition began picking up signals. "Well," she asked elliptically, "have you changed your mind?"

"No, No," Bert protested shaking his head. "I don't know if I can say what I want to, with you all gussied up, looking like a million bucks. You'll think I'm saying it because of the way you look." His voice trailed off.

The waitress was back with their orders. She topped Bert's coffee and asked if Alice wanted more hot water. She didn't. Bert said a short grace and they ate in silence. Bert was chewing his insides along with his Reuben. He was miserable. He felt like a tongue-tied rube. Alice would leave for New York, and the way she looked, men would be chasing her; what chance did he have?

Alice came to the rescue. "You said you wanted to talk to me about something long before you saw me without my disguise. Have you changed your mind? Bert, I have a plane to catch, so talk."

This was a new Alice speaking so confidently. If he didn't state his case she'd be gone and he'd be left nursing procrastination. Bert put fear of rejection aside, swallowed some coffee along with his pride, and began. "Well, I wanted to see you before you left and ask if you'd consider going out with me socially when you came back from New York. Aw heck, Alice, you've been on my mind lately...making me think of marriage, but as long as you had a husband, I couldn't say anything." He looked up from studying his coffee, into her eyes.

Her nose was turning pink and moisture was gathering in her eyes. When a couple tears escaped and ran down her cheeks, he was at her side, she was in his arms. Cradling her, he murmured, "Honey it's okay. I should've waited till you got over George's death before throwing myself at you. But I was scared you'd meet some old flame back home and decide to stay there. I couldn't stand the thought of not seeing you again, Alice. Sweetheart everything will work out for you in New York. I'm praying that things will."

She buried her head in his chest and finally stopped crying. Taking a handkerchief from him, she wiped her eyes, blew her nose, and straightened up. Bert removed himself to his own bench, blushing at his gaucheness, and waited for her to speak.

Alice demurred, she knew her answer, but a woman likes to hold out as long as she deems it safe. "I'll let you know Bert. I'll think and pray about it while I'm gone; is that alright?"

"Hey," he grinned across at her. "That's the best I could've hope for. I was afraid your answer would be a resounding NO! After all, I'm no prize rooster; just a smitten one." He laughed out of sheer relief. "Honey, you'll never have to worry about being mistreated by this guy. I'll treat you as the queen you are; and take care of you, royally." His speech sounded corny but by then he was feeling gallant and alpha male. He reached for her hands and brought them to his lips.

The waitress appeared with the dessert menu. Alice shook her head at the inference. "We're fine," Bert grinned. "She's skipping dessert, and I've already had mine," he said winking at Alice. "We're ready to go—could you bring a doggie bag along with the check? I'm too full to finish my sandwich." The waitress nodded, left, and was back shortly with box and bill. Bert left a larger than usual tip, waited till Alice slid out of the booth, and followed her to the cashier's station.

Passing some booths on their way out they failed to notice Evelyn and Brent Wade in one of them. Evelyn's sharp eyes didn't miss the duo as they passed by. She gasped and grabbed Brent's arm viciously.

"Hey, that hurts," her husband protested. "What on..."

"Look," she hissed. "You see what I see?"

Brent, rubbing his arm, craned his neck and grinned. "Well, well, our dull pastor does have a life on the other side of the pulpit. Hubba, hubba, not a bad looking lady."

"She kinda looks familiar, but I can't remember where I've seen her before," fretted Evelyn.

"Well, I'd know if I'd seen that woman before. Our old traditionalist has at least an eye for beauty. And, Pastor's enjoying his lady friend's company."

Bert and Alice stopped at her car. Before opening the driver's door for her, he cleared his throat and mumbled, "Do you think you could spare a guy a goodbye kiss...to remember you till you're back?" He grinned sheepishly down at her.

Alice blushed and raised her lips to meet his. Bert had intended to brush her lips lightly, but once his arms went around her and felt her nearness, nature took over. With Alice locked in his arms, Bert kissed her with a passion he'd forgotten existed. Alice was in tears when she broke from the embrace. This was the kind of love she'd dreamed of but had never experienced with George.

Al Green, driving in search of a parking spot, braked suddenly; his wife Jill blurted, "Hey, watch it, for pity sakes, the kids are in the back!" Al pulled into the nearest space, turned off the engine, and whistled. "Did you see what I just saw or was it a mirage?" he asked Jill.

"What?" demanded his aggrieved wife, turning to see if the kids were okay.

"I just saw our Reverend Davenport mooching a long kiss from a woman back there."

"Where? Where?" Jill's body contorted to get a glimpse of the phenomena. Bert had just withdrawn his arms from Alice, but a delighted grin lingered on his face, enough to announce that something monumental had taken place. "My goodness, my stars," exclaimed Jill Green. "Sure that's our preacher, Al?"

"You kidding? Of course it's our man of the cloth." He began to laugh. "Just wait till I tell those antsy deacons burning midnight oil trying to figure out how to run Pastor out of town."

"C'mon Al, the preacher's got a right to a love life, like the rest of you guys. No need to give that bunch of malcontents more bile to use against the preacher."

Al shrugged dismissively. "We'll see. Let's get some food to chew on while I decide whether or not to pass along this juicy tidbit to certain itching ears. He laughed derisively. His wife scowled at him, and shook her head.

Bert rescued his doggy bag from the top of Alice's car before she drove away. He was happier than he'd been in years in spite of church problems. Let 'em come, he mused. Hallelujah, God had chosen him a helpmeet. If God was for him, it didn't matter who was against him.

Alice tooted her horn, looked in her rearview mirror at Bert before exiting right, into the road traffic. "Oh God," she breathed through tears, "thank you for giving me a man who loves me."

High on euphoria, Bert all but danced to his car. Instead of going home, he headed for the mall. "This old man's gotta get new threads; can't court a woman like Alice in these old duds."

CHAPTER SIX

Alice got her first shock at the airport; her seating arrangement had been changed. "Mrs. Darlington, you've been upgraded to first class," the desk clerk informed her. "Do you have luggage to check in?"

"I don't understand," protested Alice. "I didn't order any change."

The clerk checked a computer for clarification. "The change was made and paid for by the office of Albert Thornton, Attorney at Law." The clerk was bemused at the expression on Alice's face. Alice shrugged and took the proffered boarding pass. "Much nicer accommodations," smiled the clerk. Alice nodded.

Alice called Mona. "I'm at the airport waiting to board. Would you believe it...George's lawyer upgraded me to first class. Did you tell him to?"

"Absolutely not; why would I do that? He's very anxious to meet you, hopefully in his office first thing Monday morning."

"Well, he'll have to wait till Tuesday. I've got too many things planned for the weekend and Monday. Getting myself back into what is called normal is one of them. Did you get our hotel accommodations, Mona?"

"No, Mr. Thornton did. We're booked at the Ritz Carlton. His office is footing the bill."

"What's going on, Mona? First class flight, billeted at the Ritz. What am I walking into?"

"Don't look a gift horse in the mouth right now, Allison. You need a luxury break. We can sort out the cost later. I can hardly wait to see you, Allie. It's been seven years." Mona was crying. Alice was in tears when she closed her cell to answer the boarding call.

The flight was short. Alice's thoughts of Bert and his awkward proposal swallowed up the hours. She smiled and hugged herself remembering the astonishment on his face when the "new" Alice slid into his booth at

Charlie's. She had loved Bert for years, even before his wife's death. He was the man she'd dreamed of meeting and marrying, long before George.

Mona was waiting at the bottom of the down escalator. They fell into each other's arms and sobbed openly. Passersby shrugged, smirked or looked askance at two women embracing in public. Mona moaned at Allison's added weight. "But honey, you're here...that's all that matters."

They bypassed Luggage and exited the airport. A Ritz Carlton limo chauffeur was holding a card, "Allison Darlington." He saw them approach, opened the back doors, escorted both women into the limo, and placed Allison's overnight bag on the front seat. It was nice to ride in style, bask in the ambience of luxury. Registration taken care of, they were escorted to the hotel's penthouse suite by the manager. He bowed and scraped, seeking their approval of the gorgeous suite, before making his departure. The women thanked him profusely.

"I'm at a loss to understand all this fuss Thornton's making. I'm sure George painted a scurrilous picture of me as a runaway wife causing him pain and costing him a fortune trying to find me. Something's going on that I'm not privy to."

"Well, enjoy your ignorance. At least we'll have the weekend to relax and just talk. I told Mr. Thornton you wouldn't be available till Tuesday. He wasn't happy, but I said it was your decision."

Sophisticated Allison Darlington, Titian hair coifed by an artist; dressed by New York's finest fashion designer, entered the law offices of Thornton, Blake and Prescott first thing Tuesday morning. Albert Thornton, Attorney at Law, rose from behind his impressive desk, came around to meet her with an outstretched hand. Allison shook his hand firmly and sat in the chair he indicated to her. He glanced surreptitiously again at the woman seated across from him. Not at all the type he'd imagined from George's description.

Thornton rearranged his thinking about how to handle his late client's runaway wife. The embarrassed silence grew until he cleared his throat and started the conversation in his courtroom voice. "It's good to finally meet you, Mrs. Darlington. I wish we could have met under more pleasant circumstances, but, in spite of my late client's efforts, he was unable to locate you."

Thornton averted his eyes, shuffled papers on his desk before continuing. "The untimely death of your dear husband has put you in an enviable position as far as his estate is concerned. In spite of the prolonged separation, you are his sole beneficiary."

Allison looked at him blankly, not knowing where this was going. Thornton's body language and his tone of condescension left her little doubt that he disapproved of her. Allison rose abruptly to her feet, causing Thornton to look up and gawp. She'd come to the city to take care of George's remains, not to be lectured to by a supercilious man who knew nothing about the real George Darlington's sadism. Allison reached for her large pocketbook at her feet, determined to end the conference, when Thornton rose to his feet, extending his hands.

"Please Mrs. Darlington...I am embarrassed. Have I offended you? Please sit down, there's so much to tell you."

She remained standing, until the lawyer persuaded her to be seated. She complied but was determined to set the record straight. "Your condescending manner offends me, Mr. Thornton. You know nothing about me, nor why I ran from your late client. George Darlington was a sadist. I ran from him because he threatened to kill me, twice. My last night in New York he locked me in the basement and refused to let me out till the next morning. I had been reduced to a shell of myself trying to please his every whim. He demanded I give up my job as office manager of Baxter and Olsen; threatened that he would make up a story that I was mentally ill. He insulted my friends when they called. He threatened to have me committed if I tried to leave or divorce him. When the opportunity came, I bolted. I went south and for seven years I've existed on minimum wage. I had money in both savings and checking accounts which George used as bait to track me down, if I used them. He had investigators search for me; I lived under the radar all those years. I have returned to bury him, and then I'll return south." She was shaking.

Thornton was astonished. This woman showed no signs of paranoia, spoke coherently; no subterfuge detected. Thornton's mind registered the name of the firm she'd worked for; that was a start at verifying her work record and her personality.

Allison broke into his reverie. "If you give me the name of the mortuary that has his body, I'll begin making arrangements for his cremation."

The usually verbose attorney said gently, "Please Mrs. Darlington, bear with me. This is shocking news to me. But we have much to discuss concerning your late husband's affairs. Let me have my secretary bring in coffee; it will do us both good." He smiled benignly and Allison relented, and nodded. He called his secretary. "Vera, please bring us coffee and perhaps a snack. Thank you." Vera, a salt and pepper brunette, complied. Sensing tension in her boss's office, she switched on her intercom and recorded the balance of the interview.

Thornton found refuge in pouring coffee, handing a china mug to Allison, who sat stiffly across from him. When he finally spoke, his voice was conciliatory, almost humble. "Mrs. Darlington, I confess I judged you on the strength of misinformation George gave me. It was a judgment I had no right to entertain before hearing your side of the story. Please accept my deepest apology." He looked contrite, anxious to make amends.

Allison waved her hand dismissively and took a sip of coffee before replying. "No reason for you not to judge me, knowing George's manipulative ways; you had never met me. If you don't mind, I'd like to lay aside everything and discuss George's funeral. He was adamant about cremation; hated funerals, hated churches. What mortuary was his body taken to?"

"Franklin Funeral Parlor on 57th and Chandler. The mortician is anxious to meet you to ascertain your wishes concerning his burial." Thornton pushed a card across the desk to Allison. She reached out and read it.

She shook her head. "On second thought, I'd rather have your office take care of the arrangements. I have no desire to go to the mortuary; no intention of viewing his body, nor keeping his ashes." Her face was grave; her tone flat, resolute.

Thornton lowered his eyes; he was surprised at her decisiveness. Clearing his throat, he said, "We can take care of all the arrangements, just let us know exactly what you want done. Do you want a service before the cremation?"

Allison shook her head. "George abhorred anything religious; he would have wanted to be cremated without any service."

"Your late husband's siblings are anxious to meet with you." Thornton saw tension as a variety of expressions flitted across her face. He waited.

She spoke without emotion, her words resolute. "Under no circumstances will I meet with them. The family resemblance is uncanny. I met them only twice during our marriage, and both meetings were creepy and uncomfortable. Convey my condolences to them; tell them they can have their brother's ashes. I have nothing to say to them, nor am I interested in anything they have to say to me."

Albert Thornton had not expected to be burying his late client or delivering such messages to his siblings. But, Thornton wanted to maintain Allison Darlington as a client. "Be assured that our office will attend to everything you request. You have only to let us know of any changes you have in mind."

Allison picked up the purse she'd placed on the floor beside her. "Please keep an account of the cost of what I've asked your firm to do. I will see that you are reimbursed in full."

Once more she prepared to rise. Thornton raised his hand. "Please, please...there is much more to discuss, Mrs. Darlington."

A thousand-watt bulb lit up the recesses of Thornton's brain when Allison mentioned she'd be paying for the funeral. Was it possible that this woman knew nothing about the wealth she'd inherited? He glanced at the folder on his desk, cleared his throat, and looked over at her. In a firm voice he said bluntly, "Money will never be a problem for you, Mrs. Darlington. Your late husband was an extremely wealthy man; probably a billionaire if all assets were counted."

Allison stared blankly at him, wondering if she'd heard correctly. He nodded in answer to her look of incredulity. Without warning Allison's head begin to swim and nausea attacked her stomach. She held to the edge of the desk, then put her head down to fight off the urge to vomit. Shame followed the rejection she felt by a husband who'd despised her to the point that even family finances had been hidden from her. George always had money; he was considered an excellent stockbroker. She had ceased shopping for personal items, hoping her frugality would earn her brownie points; they hadn't.

To Thornton's dismay, Allison Darlington, heiress to a huge fortune, was weeping quietly at the corner of his desk. "Vera, bring a glass of water. Mrs. Darlington is not well."

Allison roused herself after sipping the water. She nodded her thanks to Vera. After wiping her eyes and blowing her nose, Allison's composure returned. "I am so sorry for such a display of histrionics. I'd no idea what our financial status was. All I knew was that George worked for an investment firm."

Albert shook his head disgustedly. "My dear lady, George didn't work for the firm, he owned it, and three branch offices in other states. He has businesses overseas as well. He died an extremely wealthy man. It is beyond my comprehension that a husband would keep his wife in total ignorance regarding their finances. Marriage is a partnership in all things."

Thornton went on. "The deceased was insured for one million dollars, double indemnity in case of accidental death. I contacted the insurance company; there is nothing to contest. He was killed in an automobile accident. I took the liberty of acting as your attorney; asked the insurance company to deposit $50,000 in your savings account and $25,000 in your checking account. I hope you approve of what I did. Not knowing your financial status, I figured you might be in need of ready cash. The balance of the two million dollars is in a safety deposit box in your bank, at your disposal."

Allison looked over at the attorney. "Thanks for handling the money so expediently. Yes, I can use ready cash. I've existed on so little for seven years, that it will be difficult to spend money. Poor George. He spent all his life working, planning, gathering. We didn't even have a honeymoon. He was a driven man, had no time for life, only time for work, and malicious cruelty. Ironic, isn't it that he should leave as beneficiary the wife he married to destroy!" Thornton nodded, marveling at the acuity of Darlington's personality.

She suddenly laughed. "Now I know why you could afford to fly me first class and put us up at the Ritz Carlton. You know, Mr. Thornton, the scripture that came to mind when Mona told me how George died?"

He shook his head, startled at her reference to the Bible.

"'They that live by the sword, die by the sword.' I couldn't get that scripture out of my mind. Cruelty was George's specialty, and I understand his death was extremely horrible." She shook her head, and rose to her feet. She wanted to get out of the office and back to Mona. There were too many things she had to do before returning home to Bert.

Thornton stalled her departure by remarking, "Now that you've invoked the spiritual, let me share something providential with you. Two weeks ago, George called this office setting up an appointment to sign the new will he had me draw up for him. It left all his worldly possessions to his three siblings. You were cut out entirely. Inasmuch as that will was never signed, the old will stands. You are the legal heir to all he possessed." Albert Thornton looked at Allison for reaction.

She sat down quietly, his words resonating through her psyche. She finally nodded and said simply, "God had a reason for keeping that from happening. The money will be used for good. I want to know all about the monetary value of the company, and how it operates." A long pause ensued before Allison spoke again; when she did the lawyer's assessment of her character rose exponentially.

"I'd like you to bequeath money or stocks, bonds, to George's siblings. You decide how much to appropriate under these circumstances. Add a provision that none of them contact me. If they attempt to communicate in any way, the bequeaths will be withdrawn."

The lawyer nodded. "I understand; be assured that everything you've delineated here will be taken care of. Our firm, if you retain us, will handle your affairs with utmost discretion and loyalty. Your interests will be our concern."

Allison paused, giving the lawyer cause for alarm. "I think we understand each other now, Mr. Thornton, so let's continue as in the past; your firm representing Darlington Enterprises."

The lawyer, much more relaxed, escorted her to the door. Allison thanked Vera for the glass of water, wished them good day, and was gone.

Albert Thornton stood looking at the closed door. "Vera," he said turning before entering his office. "You won't believe the assassination George Darlington's character underwent by the woman that just shut that door. Unbelievable! Before I give too much credence to her story, check her out. She said that she worked as office manager for Baxter and Olson, a brokerage firm, before marrying Darlington. Her maiden name was Evans, Allison Evans."

Vera nodded. "I never liked Darlington; he gave me the creeps. I felt the presence of evil whenever he came into the office."

He looked at her in amazement. "You never mentioned anything like that to me, Vera."

"It wasn't my place to voice negative observations about your clients," she said curtly.

He shrugged and closed his office door. Women! he thought plaintively. How could mere man figure out a woman's uncanny intuition?

Vera was back with a typed statement regarding Allison Evans' work record. Allison Evans was a paralegal, had worked as office manager until her marriage to George Darlington. Owned stock in the company. Albert Thornton half expected Allison to have gilded the lily for impressions' sake. A clearer view of Allison's nature caused the lawyer to reach for the phone and begin fulfilling his obligation to his new client—that of burying her estranged husband.

Mr. Blake, the mortician, listened to Thornton's instructions carefully. "No problem, the widow's wishes will be carried out. Sorry I won't have the pleasure of meeting her. But, give Mrs. Darlington our sympathy for her loss."

CHAPTER SEVEN

Ruth Anderson brought Bert's coffee and a stack of pink telephone messages. "Morning Ruth."

"Morning Pastor; seems like the whole congregation wants to talk to you this morning, some to the point of demanding YOU return their call. Something up I'm not privy to?"

As they talked, Mike barged into the office, eyes blazing, hair on the wild side. He ignored his wife and looked balefully at Bert sitting swiveling in his chair, side to side, a silly grin on his face. "Hey, Mike, you're scaring Ruthie and I might add, me, too. Calm down, man...what's up?" Ruth left to answer her office phone; but not before glaring at her husband and shaking her head.

Mike ignored the pastor's banter, and pointed his right index finger at him and shook it at Bert. "You're what's up, Bert. If you had to kiss some lady, why on earth would you do it in the middle of Charlie's parking lot?! My entire morning's been spent playing defense, assuring our nosy congregation that maybe she's your sister, cousin, whatever; and you'll fill in the blanks later."

Bert looked over at Mike benignly and shook his head. "Sorry you've had to bear the brunt of my seeming indiscretion. And Mike I'm grateful for your loyalty. Don't know what I'd do without you."

Mike sighed, but praises didn't mitigate his angst. He'd heard enough calls for Pastor's resignation to put the wind up him. The denunciations were from staunch church members upset with news of Bert's public display of amour.

Bert looked at his young song leader and said gently, "Mike, let me assure you...this isn't what it looks like. You're worrying needlessly. Sit down; time to have a heart to heart."

Mike sat down heavily on the chair across from Bert, tired and disconsolate. Knives were already poised at the preacher's back. Now Bert himself had handed them the smoking gun.

"I can't deny kissing her, Mike. I had no idea we had an audience, but I doubt that that would have mattered. Just in case my members have forgotten, I'm single and over 18. My lady had just agreed to consider me future husband material, and I was ecstatic." He looked over at a wide-eyed Mike and clapped his hands gleefully. "You see, Mike...I'm in love. And I don't care who knows it."

A flabbergasted Mike protested. "But...but...c'mon Bert, you've never dated to my knowledge or appeared interested romantically in anyone since Jenny." Mike rose to his feet unable to take the news sitting down.

Bert brought his body forward and leaned across his desk. "Sit down, Mike, you make me nervous standing over me. There's nothing to worry about. I'm going to let you in on a secret. Of course you'll share it with Ruthie, but she'll have to keep it quiet too."

Mike nodded vigorously. "Of course."

Bert grinned. "When I have the lady's consent, I'll make a formal announcement to the church about our intended nuptials. Incidentally, everyone knows the lady in question. You've known her for years. You still work beside her as a matter of fact." Mike's face took on such facial contortions that Bert was in a paroxysm of laughter.

"C'mon Bert, be serious. Who've I worked beside that you took a shine to, or dated on the sly? From what I hear the woman in question is a catch."

"Oh she is, she is, that I can truly vouch for. You'd never recognize her, Mike, since she shed her camouflage." Mike was eager now to hear the punch line. Bert laughed, sensing his expectation.

"I'm talking about our Alice, Mike. Minus her Mother Hubbard garb, she's one good-looking woman. She's a knockout; a pure joy to look at. I'm one lucky guy. Right now she's in New York burying the husband she's been hiding from, which is why she dressed like a bag lady all this time. The guy's dead, so she's free to surface and resume her true identity, and I'm free to declare my feelings for her."

Bert reached and took a sip of cold coffee, grimaced, and looked to see how Mike was taking the news. Mike had a silly grin on his face as he mouthed. "Alice, our Alice...of all people." He stood to his feet and reached across the desk for Bert's hand. "What a story! Believe me, Bert, I thought you'd bought your own one-way ticket out of Fair Haven Church." He laughed delightedly. "The congregation'll eat this up and line up behind you. Everyone who's come in contact with Alice loves her. But what are you going to do until you can reveal the truth?"

"I'll think of something, don't fret over that. String the congregation along with vague remarks and innuendoes. Don't forget I've got your Ruthie manning the phone to keep the natives cool and comfortable."

"Wow," said Mike, "what a revelation to what I thought was your last meal here. Yeah, Ruthie's great at subterfuge. But don't tell her I said that." He laughed conspiratorially, and Bert winked.

"Well lover boy," said Mike, "yours truly has gotta go and make some dollars for a family that can't stop eating and feet that can't stop growing." Mike bounded out of Bert's office. He heard him call, "Ruthie, you aren't going to believe this!" If a man had to share news who better to share it with than his wife?

The phone rang off the desk, off the wall, off of every place an electronic gadget could find purchase. Bert turned the calls over to Ruth and grinned as she, with great aplomb, tackled indignant members' queries about pastor's great indiscretion.

"Would you agree Pastor has a right to a life outside of church?" "Rev. Davenport is a single man." "Pastor's conduct has always been above reproach." "Rev. Davenport will address this situation if he deems it necessary." "For pity's sake...this is the 21st century." The phone rang all day. Bert stood at Ruthie's door, watched her flushed face, and mouthed, "I'm out of here," holding up hospital notes. She nodded, gave him a thumbs' up, and got back to pouring oil over irate congregants. Bert thought how lucky Mike was to have a wife like Ruth; indeed, she was a pearl of great price.

Nature did its best to sweeten D-Day for the reluctant chauffeurs assigned to chaperone the teens delivering flyers. The bright morning, the cool breezes, and the singing birds did little to dispense of the drivers' angst. They'd been deprived of that golf game, fishing trip, or tinkering around with that vintage car. If that meddlesome preacher hadn't saddled them with HIS responsibility, they'd be doing their Saturday thing. And HE had the audacity to turn up missing. Hadn't bothered coming to witness their bit of work for the Lord. What a jerk!

Before leaving for New York, Alice cautioned, "Bert, stay clear of the church till the flyer operation is over. You'll be their straw horse if you're there." Contrary to his past inclinations, Bert followed her advice. Scott Martin called later with the rundown of the day's events.

"How did it go, Scott?" Bert asked when Scott phoned.

Laughter was Scott's answer, before using prose. "It was like a Laurel and Hardy movie at first, preacher. All the deacons showed up. Hunt brought his teenage daughter who sat in the car playing on her phone till he dragged her bodily out of the car and I teamed her with another girl. Twelve kids showed up; two for six cars. The seventh deacon thought he was going to sit out the morning, but Mike showed up, so he and I did some streets. He was barely civil when we got into his Mercedes. After a while our deacon felt the urge to ply his faith and do some porch climbing for the Lord. He joined in, huffing and puffing up and down the steps like the rest of us. When we all got back to the church, the mood had changed dramatically. The men actually enjoyed stretching their legs instead of their tongues. Hunt took the gang to McDonald's, paid the whole tab. He'll probably put it down to business expense, but who cares. I'd say they had a good time all around. But you were wise to stay away. At the beginning some of the guys had blood in their eyes...wanted to know where YOU were." Scott chuckled, and added, "I would chalk it up to a good day of bonding, preacher. Those deacons will sleep better tonight, not because of the exercise, but because they put forth some effort to get this show on the road. I guess that covers everything, unless you have questions?"

"No, no, Scott. Just glad you were there to handle what I couldn't. See you Sunday. Good day. God bless."

Alice didn't call until Wednesday. By then Bert was walking the floor, chewing his nails along with his gut. He ignored the inner voice cautioning, "Trust the Lord, Bert." His imagination had soared to unbelievable heights. Alice had met an old flame; probably out dining...calling Bert was an imposition. When she did call it would be to tell him she'd changed her mind about them. And, who could blame her? What did he have to offer her anyway? That's when the phone rang.

"Alice! Alice," his voice went up a notch when he heard her voice. "I was afraid you'd changed your mind about keeping in touch."

"No, no, Bert. I've been busy, busy, busy with funeral arrangements; meeting with George's attorney, settling his affairs. Plus getting a real estate agent to handle my house. Mona's helping me with that chore. I'll have to come back to sort out and tag paintings and furnishings, and mark the furniture I want to keep before the estate sale. I hadn't forgotten you Bert, but my plate's so full of demands for my time. By the way, can you recommend a good storage company where I can send the things I want to keep to Safe Haven?"

Bert was relieved; Alice was making plans to come back. "No need for that, honey, my basement's dry and pretty empty. It'll hold any furniture, and whatever you send down. The address is 4114 Springer Avenue, Safe Haven, South Carolina. And honey, ship yourself to that address posthaste. This old guy's missing you." His voice dropped a decibel. Alice heard its alter and sighed. How would Bert take the news that she was now a very rich widow? Would it change the dynamics of things? Instead of him looking after her, she'd be in a position of looking after him. She barricaded that road and took a side road to other matters.

"Incidentally," said Bert laughing, "you are presently referred to as Pastor's mystery woman. Seems like some of our members caught sight of me kissing you in Charlie's parking lot. Phones of all shapes and vintage have been ringing nonstop. If they could hang the scarlet letter 'A' around my neck, I do believe they'd try." He laughed uproariously at the thought of that being tried.

Alice felt her face flush as she remembered that kiss. Changing the subject she asked. "How're preparations going for the Faulkner meeting?"

"Well, it's been a long time since the church has had such a cleansing, so that's a plus. Everyone's pitching in, tackling dust and cobwebs with brushes, soap and polish. What's got me in a dither is that I've yet to meet Faulkner. He's in a meeting out of state; won't be in South Carolina till the Sunday morning he's to speak. It's a predicament I've never encountered before, knowing less than nothing about the speaker's doctrine, or what he looks like. I tell you Alice, I don't want to be caught like Jacob, with the wrong bride behind the veil, and too late to say no deal. The deacons' sketchy outline of his message does little to calm my nerves. In essence he'll be addressing the need for traditional churches to bring their doctrines to the 21st century; you know, get acquainted with today's culture and leave the past behind, etc. Hopefully he'll get here early Sunday. But even so, if I wanted to stop him from preaching, I'd do more harm than good. It's a catch twenty-two. No pun intended, but I may be put on a Greyhound bus after his spiel. Or, Faulkner could leave me the headache of fulfilling all the pipe dreams he blows out to our people about getting millennials into church by getting rid of orthodox Christianity. It's a stretch...but then my mind is stretching to the ridiculous. It's all in God's hands."

Bert was no stranger to church splits. Splits were born at the drop of a hat, a shoe, a word, a fancied slight, a whim. Heinz's 57 had no corner on the number of tastes a split could develop from. "Honey, I apologize for sounding petulant. Wish you were here. Your presence gives me what I need: comfort and assurance. I love you so much; want to do so much for you...and I will...that, you can take to the bank."

Alice winced at the mention of bank, and disconnected at the first opportunity. Her mind went from Bert to the next man she was scheduled to meet, David Carpenter, CFO of Darlington Enterprises. She'd spoken to him over the phone; what would he be like in person?

CHAPTER EIGHT

David Carpenter listened, shrugged, covered the phone's mouth piece and whispered into the intercom... "Coffee." Albert Thornton was finishing his peroration regarding the Darlington widow. David took the coffee from his secretary, mouthed thanks, and took a sip as he continued listening.

"So where's this lady been hiding all these years?"

"Down South, working for minimum wage; low profile...scared George's investigators would find her."

"Yeah, yeah, well I know George spent a bundle trying to track her down. C'mon Al, do you believe her? No question about George being quirky, the guy was a work freak...had no time for her, so she scarpered off, but not without draining his ATM and savings account. I mean, do you think she's the kind who'd make up the marriage in hell scenario to justify running out on old George?" He waited for Thornton's reply as he sipped his coffee.

"David, she's one shrewd businesswoman; worked at Baxter as office manager; has a paralegal degree. She wants you to bring her up to speed regarding George's business holdings. From all indications, she knew nothing about George's wealth; thought he was a stockbroker, period. She wants to meet with the executives in charge of overseas operations. If any of you think you're in clover with the big guy gone, think again. Allison Darlington is a woman you'd better take seriously. If she's got something in her craw about the company...it'll happen. George controlled the company with built-in protection to ward off any coup. His paranoia will serve her well as it did him.

"My pro bono advice: call Mrs. Darlington, set up the meet she wants. As for me, I'm up to my chin with burial arrangements for the dearly departed George Darlington. She wants nothing to do with the body, no intention of viewing his remains, nor taking home the ashes."

"Thanks, I hear you. What about Darlington's siblings?" Carpenter asked before ending the conversation. "See any problems coming from that end?"

"None. The will's sound; she gets the whole bundle; she's sole beneficiary."

"You don't think they'll try to contest it, seeing she was an estranged wife for almost seven years?"

"Not a chance. If they took her to court, George's character would be trashed. She can verify her hiding place, her penurious living conditions; her fear of George trying to kill her. Not even those creepy siblings would want that aired. Let me know how you get along with Allison Darlington." He recited her cell number before they ended the call.

It was Saturday, 4 p.m., when Bert drove into the church parking lot to find a multitude of cars. "Looks like a Wednesday night meeting," he mused aloud. After checking his messages, he left his office and headed in the direction of all the commotion, laughter, and whirring of the vacuum cleaner. The caretaker's ancient Kirby was trying valiantly to pick up dirt rather than deposit it in on the worn carpet. Bert gazed lovingly at the sanctuary with its three sections of walnut pews; the middle section twice the length of the side pews. Each end was painted white highlighting the oak carvings underneath the paint. The periwinkle blue seats and back were still in good condition.

The dark blue carpet was threadbare in many places. When the budget allows, we're going to replace this eyesore, he thought to himself. But, with offerings down, such replacements would have to wait.

Two women were busy dusting the pews while another polished the communion table, changed the linen, and placed a bowl of fresh flowers on it. Sunday evening the table would hold the elements for the Lord's Supper. He glanced at the pulpit he'd stood behind for 18 years, and prayed for the one who would stand behind it Sunday morning. The platform accommodated the choir that sat behind a white wooden knee-high barrier, his personal chair, and the pulpit. Mike had plenty of room to strut around while leading the singing. There was a door to the left used by the choir to enter the platform. Bert often used it. The piano sat to the right of the pulpit. The baptistery was on the wall behind the choir with a mural of Christ's baptism painted over it. Bert loved this church. How often he'd felt the presence of God hovering over the people as they worshiped! But lately church division had squelched feeling the Presence. Oh God, he breathed silently, Sunday bring revival to my people; we need a touch from Your Spirit.

Someone touched his sleeve: Mrs. Massingale. "Pastor," she spoke softly and he was back from his wanderings. She leaned on her walker; stooped with age, face wrinkled by time and concern. "Pastor...I don't think it's right to set aside the Lord's Supper for a speaker. We always have communion on the second Sunday morning of each quarter. I think we're getting our priorities wrong by putting the Lord off till next week."

"Not to worry Aggie," soothed the Reverend kindly. "It will give the visiting minister more time. We'll have the Lord's Supper Sunday night. I don't think the Lord's going to remove our candlestick because we accommodated a guest speaker. Our God knows what's going on, Aggie. Not to worry."

She was less than mollified. "I don't know preacher; I think this guy's going to stir up trouble, trouble that's already brewing. What do you think, preacher?"

Traps come in all sizes, colors, and disguises. Bert had been visited by all varieties and was wary of even members wearing angelic countenances. "Let's just wait and see, we may learn something profitable, Aggie."

He left after patting her shoulder, but not before he heard her say, "Yes Pastor, but I'm afraid it'll be something we can well do without."

Sunday dawned; joy unspeakable and full of glory! The sun shone, birds chirped, soft breezes caressed, no hint of rain; almost 70 degrees. Bert stood at his office window watching family after family drive into the parking lot, disgorge passengers and move to park the car. Kids raced toward other kids before entering the building. He remembered Sundays when families presented themselves in God's house in their Sunday best. He thought of his mom laying out Sunday clothes Saturday night; shoes polished, shirts, dresses, ironed for church. Dad's trousers had a new crease, even though the seat of his pants shone. Yeah, he mused, they were poor but rich in what counted. Sunday was Sunday school and church; Bibles in hand. Dinner was cooking while they sang songs of Zion. Church may have bored them as kids, but they learned to sit and listen, knowing Mom was a short distance away ready to pinch leg or arm of any kid misbehaving. Bert grinned and rubbed his arm, remembering pinches he frequently acquired in church.

Returning to the present, Bert found himself fighting for identity. Where did he belong this morning? He felt like a kid upstaged by the arrival of a new baby in the house. A knock on his door; Mike stuck his head in. "Time to go Pastor, can't get the show on the road without the main guy behind the pulpit."

Bert grinned. Count on Mike to know what to say and when to say it. He and Jenny had taken him in, when, at 15, Mike's estranged father had shot Mike's mother, then himself. It was Mike who'd found the bodies when he came home from high school. Reverend Davenport worked with social workers diligently to get Mike placed in their home, where he was treated like one of the Davenport kids. Mike's oldest son was named after Bert. The memory of that transition, Mike never forgot. He owed his present status to Bert and Jenny Davenport.

Bert nodded weakly. "Yeah, guess I'm as ready as any lamb ever is, trotting to the slaughter." He laughed and patted Mike's shoulder as they made their way to the hall leading to the sanctuary.

Both auditorium doors were wide open as people poured in from Sunday school, greeting friends while heading for their favorite pew. Creatures of habit...we feel comfortable in that special place in church, relieved when we find it unoccupied.

Mike made his way to check with Sylvia, the pianist, then darted to the choir room to the left of the pulpit. Bert lingered at the back of the auditorium, watching the congregation. He recognized members who'd been absent for years. It'll be a full house, he mused, wistfully remembering that this was how it was when he and Jenny came as pastor and wife years ago. Many, like Jenny, had gone to meet their Maker; others had just lost interest in church. Why? Perhaps Faulkner's data would identify why traditional churches are losing members, closing church doors. Did Faulkner have a magic formula that would stem the tide of the spiritual erosion going on? If so, Bert would gladly welcome his advice.

Bert spied Faulkner right away, surrounded by the deacons. A broth of a man, Bert's Highland grandmother would have labeled him. Tall, silver headed, sans facial hair. He wore an expensive custom-made charcoal jacket, light gray slacks, dazzling white shirt and a multi-colored silk tie that completed the sartorial picture. Bert felt outdated in his three-piece navy suit, white shirt, conventional tie.

Chastening himself for being morose, Bert walked down the far aisle to where Faulkner and his deacons were laughing congenially. Holding out his hand he quipped in a jocular tone, "Dr. Livingston I presume? We finally meet."

Faulkner understood the inference, smiled, extended his hand, and apologized. "I beg your forgiveness Pastor Davenport, for not meeting with you before this, but my lousy schedule prevented me from doing so. You are more than gracious to allow me to speak to your people under such circumstances." Faulkner's apology and smile were sincere. Common sense told Bert at this juncture there was nothing to be done but let the man speak his piece.

Bert waved the apology aside. "You're here...that's all that matters. My parishioners are anxiously waiting to hear your message." While Bert talked with the evangelist, he walked with him away from the deacons. "We'll have time to chat at the dinner the deacons have planned for you after the service."

At the edge of the platform, Bert explained, "I'll make the regular announcements and recognize your presence, and Bob Billingsly will introduce you to the congregation. I have no idea what your message is, but I will be praying for you, brother." He shook the evangelist's hand, pointed him to the middle front pew; Faulkner sat down. Bert ascended the platform on rubbery legs.

Mike came over to Bert immediately. "Anything I should know before I get this show on the road?"

Bert shook his head. "No. It's all yours, Mike. Pray for the speaker." Bert sat down on his platform chair, and prayed.

Mike nodded to the pianist. Sylvia came down heavy on the keys. The choir took its place; the people rose at Mike's gesture. Mike led in prayer, invoking the Holy Spirit to honor them with His presence. "Amen," concluded Mike. "Turn to page 134, 'Redeemed, How I Love to Proclaim It!' Sing like you mean it. Bring down heaven." Smiles from the folk as they opened mouths and sang as one voice the song of redemption. *Redeemed, redeemed, redeemed by the blood of the Lamb.*

Bert listened, eyes closed. Oh God, he breathed...I need power from on high to lead this people through these troublesome times. Bert heard, amongst the male singers, the gravelly voice of Ed Brown, and tears stung his eyes. What a work God had done on that surly, uncouth individual. Only the Maker Himself could have remolded Ed Brown from what he'd been, to the kind, humble man he was today, when Ed asked Jesus to come into his heart. *Redeemed, redeemed*, sang Ed Brown. *His child and forever I am...*

Bert turned the visiting evangelist over to Bob, and gingerly made his way from platform to front pew. Feeling the sting of being maneuvered out of his pulpit, Bert diverted his angst to giving full attention to the speaker, and prayed for a calm exterior to any who kept watch on his demeanor.

"Dr. Randall Faulkner," enthused Bob Billingsly, "has been on a mission to ascertain why people are leaving traditional churches like ours." Taking a sip of water, Bob choked as he swallowed. Recovering from splutters, he continued hoarsely, "Those of us with kids are having a time keeping them in Sunday school and church. The good doctor has traveled America, listening and observing how other churches are dealing with the problems we're facing as well." Bob recited Faulkner's academic achievements, his numerous awards; how his views were sought after in church circles. Anecdotes about Dr. Faulkner had Bob on a roll until his wife caught his eye, and delivered a wife telepathy: "Enough already." Like a faucet turned off at its source, Bob shut up and reluctantly handed the eminent Faulkner the microphone. Faulkner thanked him, then directed his attention to the applauding congregation. The head deacon left the platform in the midst of the fanfare.

The evangelist lifted his right hand, nodded his thanks to the people and invited them to be seated; they complied. "Thank you, thank you," he gushed in a voice that matched his image: smooth, cultured.

"He's like a modern-day Moses," whispered a voice seated behind Bert.

Bert cringed and thought, the guy's been elevated to prophet-hood before delivering manna or quails. His inner voice accused him of being jealous. "You can't cope with sitting in the pew; you have to be behind the pulpit pontificating, or you're bent out of shape." His better nature interrupted with, "This too shall pass...hang in." Bert hung in.

Faulkner, Bert observed, knew how to keep the congregation's interest. Dry statistics became palatable as the evangelist cajoled them into the ears of the people. In a quiet voice that had the people leaning forward, he said solemnly, "Four years ago, I was approached by a group of concerned evangelical businessmen wondering why orthodox Christianity seems to be losing its relevancy and its ability to attract millennials to its services. They had a list of churches in north, south, east and west, willing to participate in the survey."

Faulkner stopped for a drink of water, cleared his throat, and continued. "I talked it over with my wife, Julie. It was fine for me, for as an evangelist I am also custodian of my time. However, leaving Julie for three, four years was a nonstarter. That problem was quickly dealt with. Julie was interested in accompanying me, and they were willing to hire her as my secretary. A contract was drawn up to both parties' satisfaction. And Julie even read the fine print." Laughter. "We were offered a generous salary plus all expenses paid. Julie's workload increased as the survey developed; recording interviews, photographing everything that moved, etc. But it was a wonderful experience for us both. We were so busy that the usual mundane bickering between spouses, almost disappeared." Laughter.

"In exchange for all of our work, we would relinquish all rights to project data in all media forms. Our research would be exclusively theirs to edit, and from which to draw their conclusions. It was a fair exchange. The committee, incidentally, is composed of eminent pastors, theologians, Christian psychologists, and learned Christian laymen, anxious to see what can be done to stem the flight from traditional churches. After a year of studying and editing our research, they have published our findings with their interpretation of it, in a book, *Orthodox Christianity Grows Young*. It's an excellent review of our fieldwork. Their conclusions you may or may not agree with, but it is well worth reading. Copies of the book are in your

Narthex. I encourage you get a copy; it delineates more information than I can possibly deliver in one lecture."

For the next forty minutes, Dr. Faulkner walked the congregation through his countless interviews with pastors caught in the dilemma of ecclesiastical culture change. The plight of the pastors, bereft of staff, that were literally keeping the doors open with aid of wife and family; ministers throwing in the towel out of sheer frustration, leaving members without a shepherd. Some preachers were even moonlighting to pay family bills, rather than take a salary from meager offerings needed to pay church bills.

"I received permission to visit members who'd once been faithful attendees, and asked why they'd stopped attending church. Regardless of what part of the country, the answers were basically the same: 'Church doesn't seem as important to us as it once was.' 'We work some Sundays.' 'We're too busy.' 'We travel a lot on weekends.' 'We work hard all week; sleep in on Sundays.' 'It's our day to golf, fish, or run.' 'When the weather's good, we take the kids to the zoo, or swimming, because it's the only day we have to do things as a family.'"

Faulkner let that information resonate through the minds of his listeners. "At one point I boldly asked a former parishioner, 'When your spirit needs a message from God, where do you turn?' I received this answer without any embarrassment, 'There's always the Internet; you can find plenty of good sermons day or night, if you need one,' was the reply."

He looked at his audience: disbelief on some faces; recognition on others. Faulkner hesitated before dumping more unpleasant information on their heads. He took refuge in a drink of water before stating, almost apologetically, "Twenty-first century millennials were often hostile in their denunciation of conservative Christian churches. They accuse traditional churches as being gloomy, not people-friendly; dwelling in archaic subjects such as the Cross, repentance, etc. Sanctuary pews, choirs, hymnals, organs, and even pianos to some are seen as artifacts of the past and should be disposed of. Preachers needed to be more hip in their appearance, cut their messages in half, talk about things that are current, rather than deal in the past. Millennials were consistent in their denunciation of hymns as too funereal. They said the sanctuary needed more light, more modernity, to keep up with the times.

"I quote from one young man; I asked how he felt after sitting listening to a sermon in a traditional church. 'I was glad to get out of there; I felt condemned, all the time the pastor was preaching. I needed fresh air after that.'"

An ambience of gloom settled over the sanctuary. Faulkner paused, then said, "I could wish my message was one of joy and happiness, but unfortunately there is a schism in Christendom today: traditionalism vs. liberalism. Ignoring the problem will not remove it. Jesus established the church; it's the human organ Christ delegated to spread the gospel of salvation to the world. The apostle Paul in Romans wrote concerning the work of the church, 'How then shall they call on Him in whom they have not believed? And how shall they believe in Him of whom they have not heard? And how shall they hear without a preacher; and how shall they preach except they be sent? As it is written, how beautiful are the feet of them that preach the gospel of peace, and bring glad tidings of good things!'"

The evangelist brought his speech to a close as he urged the parishioners to read his book, concluding, "Consider the suggestions the Committee proffers, and be apprised of what options the church has. Thank you for your attention today." He looked at Bert and nodded. He was finished. Bert signaled to Mike. Close in song and prayer; no invitation.

With the last song, prayer, and Amen, people moved toward Faulkner, who had descended from the platform. There were questions thrown his way and Bert felt sorry for him as he tried to answer them while drained and exhausted from preaching. Before Bert could reach the evangelist he heard, "Pastor, Pastor!" Ruth Anderson gestured to him as she made her way down the aisle. "Pastor, Joe Emmons just called. His dad's dying; the family's gathered in his hospital room. Joe wants you to come before his father passes. I said you'd be right there. Okay?"

Bert nodded. "Yes, yes. I'm on my way. Thanks Ruthie." Bert tapped Bob Billingsly's shoulder. "You heard Ruth?" Bob nodded. "Give my regrets to Dr. Faulkner, I doubt I'll make the dinner in his honor. Bob nodded. Bert maneuvered his way to the evangelist. "Sorry, but there's an emergency."

Faulkner nodded, "I heard."

"I'd like to spend time with you doctor. I appreciated your message. Maybe we can grab a cup of coffee later?"

Faulkner reached for Bert's hand, shook it, and said, "I'd like that."

Waiting for a loved one to cross from life to death is the hardest task we mortals face. Bert entered the room of encroaching death. Weeping and blowing of noses were the only sounds he heard. A path was cleared for him. Bert stood at the bedside and looked down at the emaciated form of John Emmons, a man who'd been one of his dependable deacons years ago. Bert's throat constricted as he murmured, "Well done thou good and faithful servant, you're going to your reward." He reached and took John's fragile left hand, the bones and knuckles visible. He could feel a whisper of a pulse as the hand rested in his. Bert bent down and said softly, "You're getting ready to meet the Lord, John." The old eyes flickered, then opened. A faint smile and an imperceptible nod followed.

Without preamble, Bert in his steady, clear voice began: "The Lord is my Shepherd, I shall not want...though I walk through the valley of the shadow of death I will fear no evil...." At that juncture, John's hand went limp in Bert's. The Lord's staff had taken over. Jesus' weary servant was home, in a land where pain, sorrow, or dying cannot enter.

Without turning his head, Bert said to John's sorrowing family, "The apostle Paul's words say it all. 'To be absent from this body is to be present with the Lord.' John's with Jesus. It's only right that we weep, for we are human and miss our loved ones. But we sorrow not as those who have no hope. For all who know Christ as Savior will meet, and be reunited with our loved ones one day. What hope, what consoling hope."

A pall of gloom rode home with Bert. Death opened memories and revived buried sorrows. Instead of stopping at a drive-through, he went home. Whatever leftovers in the fridge would supply his physical needs, appetite indifferent. He had an evening service to get through.

Bert stood looking out of his office window, watching John Whiteford amble to his old Buick, unlock the driver's side, and slide in behind the wheel. Our custodian's getting old like me, mused Bert, thinking of 18 years back when he and Jenny came. A younger John showed them around the buildings with a proprietorial air. With the church secured, the caretaker was on his way home. I should be doing the same, thought Bert, and turned when Mike came in holding coffee mugs and a couple of sorry-looking donuts on a paper plate.

"Hey, where'd you find those rejects, Mike?" He grinned, pointing at the donuts.

"Way back in the fridge, overlooked by scroungers. Don't knock 'em, they're ripe for dunking. Better'n nothing."

Bert took the coffee mug proffered him, and picked up a hard donut. "Thanks Mike. You make a mean cup of coffee," he said, sampling the brew.

"Thanks. Ruthie wouldn't agree, but since she's not here, I'll accept the compliment." Ruth had taken their three kids home after church; school came early Monday morning.

The two men sat in companionable silence, munching, drinking, thinking. "Well," began Mike, breaking the silence after swallowing coffee, "do you think Faulkner's message moved any of our people to Gregory Hunt's side?"

Bert dunked a piece of donut and shrugged negligibly. "Haven't a clue, Mike. I've been surprised too many times to even hazard a guess as to how my flock's going to react to a controversy. I can pretty well predict how our seniors will feel. But then again, Faulkner's data certainly gave them something to consider. I'll give him his due, he tried not to be biased. I'll know more about his personal convictions when I read the book.

"He was right though, there is a schism in traditional churches today; we're in the midst of one ourselves. I can feel resentment coming from some in the congregation outside of Hunt's group. Satan's at work, Mike, big time. Orthodox Christianity is struggling to maintain its position as a moral guide in the community; we're losing influence. There was a time when non-members from the community would come in for counseling; that's ceased. Even my own members are seeking counseling from secular psychologists. The clergy's become a nonentity. Think about it Mike.

How many weddings are we conducting these days? Yet people are getting married. More weddings are taking place outside the church, in halls, or gardens, etc. The leaven of liberalism is permeating every facet of Christianity. It's changing our people, Mike...changing values...changing attitudes about God. I fear for our country's future, Mike."

Mike left the office and returned with the coffee pot. Bert poured his cold coffee in a dying plant, and thanked Mike for the refill.

Sitting down, Mike asked seriously, "Where do you think Faulkner's loyalty lies, Bert? His summation was the committee's, not his own."

"I don't know, Mike. But I liked him, and I wish I'd had a chance to talk to him before he left town, but that didn't happen. I don't know what his true convictions are, because I don't know what doctrinal flag he flies under. I'm grateful that he left me in one piece, and not under the bus." Bert laughed; Mike joined in.

"Speaking of doctrine...do you know what millennials, or progressives, or emerging Christians, or whatever they call themselves, what doctrine they espouse, Bert? Faulkner didn't say."

"That's a conundrum Mike. We've discussed that issue at clergy conferences. But the best we've come up with is that they have no doctrinal base. Emerging Christians disdain theological doctrines. All they need is Jesus; no rules, instructions, etc." Bert sipped coffee and looked at Mike and sighed.

"What've they got against doctrines?"

"Well, think about it, Mike. Christian doctrines more or less emulate spiritual beliefs. In a way, doctrines are alarm clocks that go off when we leave the straight and narrow. Baptist doctrine states that we believe the biblical account of Creation; the Virgin birth; Christ's miracles; the Cross; the Resurrection; the Rapture; the Tribulation period; the Millennium. Our doctrines reflect our beliefs. They keep us God-focused, not twisting in the winds of indecision."

Mike nodded. "Yeah, I hear ya. What kind of faith do progressives or millennials hold to, if there's no certain doctrine?"

"That's something I can't answer Mike. Emergent gurus are all over the ecclesiastical map. For instance, Burke, one prominent leader, rejects the Cross as an atonement for sin. He calls himself a universalist. He doesn't believe you have to convert to any particular religion to find God.

God finds us; it has nothing to do with subscribing to any particular religious belief." Bert finished the last of his coffee.

Mike shook his head. "Wow! Do they believe in a final judgment?"

"Again, I don't know, but from what I've read, their leaders do not believe people go to hell. They aver that such a belief is contradictory to the Bible's own account of God being the epitome of Love. Scriptures are used to prove or to disprove new ideas that hit them."

"Bert, I had a time keeping my cool when Faulkner was dishing out that garbage about what Millennials thought of Christians and our churches. I wasn't the only one...I saw lots of angry faces and felt their angst, like mine, rise."

"Yeah, that was pretty brutal. Freedom of speech has become a venue used by liberals to peddle hate. It's used to voice ugly and vulgar criticism against those who hold different opinions, and shuts conservative rebuttal.

"But Mike, the flip side of Millennial denunciation of orthodox Christianity could turn on them. Our people, for the most part, were incensed at Millennials condemning our church. Those who were teetering for change, might now change their minds, not wanting to have any part of the philosophy liberals ascribe to. God works in mysterious ways, Mike."

"Oh yeah...you can say that again, padre."

Mike's cell rang. "Ruthie," he winked at Bert. "Yeah, I'm on my way; need anything from the store? The kids OK, or do they need a friendly talk from the guy that wears the black hat?" He listened, nodding all the time. "OK see you in five. Love ya."

Returning his cell to his jacket pocket, he picked up the empty cups and headed for the kitchen. "Coming, Pastor?"

Bert groaned, "Yeah, it's getting late. Don't want to be a statistic lying on the parking lot for Whiteford to find in the morning."

Mike shivered. "You never know these days, padre. A man's occupation doesn't guarantee security." Bert followed Mike, closing his office door behind him. Mike deposited the cups in the kitchen sink; they made their way to the parking lot. Bert made sure the side door was locked.

"When's Alice coming home?" Mike asked at Bert's car, watching as he opened the driver's door and slid in.

"Should be any day now, that's what she said the other night. I'll probably hear from her before the night's over. She'll want to hear about Faulkner's message."

Mike nodded. "Yeah, and I'm anxious to meet this new Alice you keep talking about." He grinned as Bert's face took on a crimson hue. Bert had it bad. "Good night Pastor." Mike tapped the roof of Bert's car and headed toward his own.

Before Mike could turn the key in the ignition his cell rang. "I'm on my way woman...give me a break. Glancing at the phone lying on the passenger's seat, he saw that the I.D. was not his wife's. "This is Mike," he began, "who..." and got no further.

"Mike, we've got to talk. Can you meet me in the office, say at 7:30 Wednesday morning? It's important."

Mike looked at his cell; who on earth?

"Mike, you there?" Light dawned; he yelped. "Alice, is that you? For goodness sake are you home?"

"No, not yet, but I will be Tuesday night. I need to talk to you before I see Bert. Can we meet?"

A wary Mike was silent. When he spoke, there was an edge in his voice. "If you're gonna tell the boss you've changed your mind about him, I'm not your pigeon. Won't help you make it easy to break his heart."

He heard aggravation before she said wearily, "Nothing like that Mike. Something's come up, and I need your advice before I talk to Bert."

Relieved, Mike answered, "Sure. I can wait for you at your place Tuesday evening...talk then if you've a mind to; check out your place before you go in."

"No, no. I'll be OK. I'll see you Wednesday morning. Thanks." She disconnected.

CHAPTER NINE

He winked at his image in the huge plate glass window; it winked back approvingly. David Carpenter pressed the button on his desk.

"Yes Sir?" his secretary responded. "What do you need?"

"Karen, you all set to tape my conversation with our distinguished guest when she gets here?"

"Oh sure, ready and listening, like a mouse. What about coffee? Bring it in when she comes, or wait for your signal?"

"Better wait, don't know if she drinks coffee, tea or whatever. I'll let you know. Just give me a heads up when she's at our doorstep."

Fifteen minutes later: "Boss, she's outside the office. Martha's getting ready to knock on your door. Have fun."

David Carpenter was on his feet when Martha ushered Allison Darlington into his large, plushy office. He advanced to meet her with an outstretched hand. "So good to finally meet you, Mrs. Darlington," he gushed. They shook hands; she took the chair he motioned her to.

"Can I offer you coffee, tea?"

Allison shook her head. "Thanks, I'm fine."

Not a good start, he thought. Perceived or real, tensions were usually mitigated with a cup of good, hot java. He was taken aback at her appearance. He'd envisioned meeting a tough middle-aged blonde, who'd left old George for another guy, and was back to claim her due as widow. The woman seated across from him was no slouch; she had class and poise, and was in her middle fifties. He wished he'd paid more attention to Thornton's assessment of her. He felt shaky in her presence; something new for the suave character he imagined himself to be. His mind told him to sit up and take note. He straightened up, and trotted out his best business manners.

A pall of silence descended; Allison broke it by retrieving a small notebook from her capacious handbag she'd placed on the floor by her chair. "I have looked up your employment record Mr. Carpenter. You've been George's CEO in charge of financial matters for 15 years?" David nodded numbly, wondering where this meeting was going. A chill of unease crept into his spine and he felt sweat accumulating under his armpits and at his hairline. No one looked on him as an employee; he was part of the company, a CEO with stock, not some lowly clerk. How dare she check his personnel file! He realized she was talking. He perked up and listened.

"For my own records, I'd like an overview of what your duties are, what your department does, the infrastructure of the business end of Darlington Enterprises. In my research of the company I understand we have foreign investments in three European countries. I would like the individuals in charge of foreign operations to be advised that I want to discuss Darlington's investments in Europe. If you will, please set up a meeting with me and the individuals involved." She smiled, taking some of the sting out of her words. "With Europe in a financial upheaval," she continued, "I am considering removing all vestiges of Darlington operations from Europe to concentrate on American investments. Please advise them of my thinking and get back to me."

David Carpenter was stunned; his tongue was dead weight in his mouth. Finally corralling his wits, he said soberly, "I will see that those involved in overseas operations are informed. The news will be a shock to them, for overseas operations are very lucrative to our company, not even taking into consideration the jobs that will be lost by closing them down."

"I'm aware of that Mr. Carpenter. Change is never pleasant; I am well acquainted with the consequences of change," she added dryly. He caught the inference. "Thank you for your service to the corporation. I hope we can continue working together."

Was that a threat, if he bucked her? He wasn't about to try that one on for size. "Be assured that your instructions will be passed on to the CEOs involved. You have my complete cooperation."

Allison rose to her feet, and David jumped on his, winding his way around the desk, escorting her to the reception area. She nodded to Martha, and vanished through the door, heading for the elevators.

Carpenter's inner door opened. Karen entered carrying coffee and sandwiches. He nodded thanks; she sat across from him and poured them coffee. Karen sat stirring hers while looking at her boss. "Wow!" she said, shaking her head. "She's some woman!"

David Carpenter put cream in his coffee, raised the cup to his lips, but couldn't swallow. Nerves had paralyzed his throat. He finally coaxed some liquid down his esophagus. "She talked to me like I was some clerk, rather than the financial head of her company."

"Oh, c'mon David. Every new broom needs sharp bristles to let the peons know they've got a new boss. Someone's gonna be watching to see if you're earning that fat salary you're being paid. We'll get the stuff she asked for, no big deal. I'll dress it up nice and neat. Once she's established her iron scepter over you guys, she'll leave town and things will go back to normal."

He looked up. "You think?"

Karen shrugged. "Yeah...I think."

Carpenter drank more coffee and mused, "Well, wish I had your optimism, but my gut tells me this dame's gonna rearrange our lives, along with the company's," he added petulantly. "Better put in a conference call to Greene, Stokes, and Stevenson. They need a heads up on this new development; need to share my misery." He grinned thinking of the three smug CEOs. Karen nodded and left his office.

Later that evening Carpenter called Allison. "I informed the CEOs in charge of overseas operations of your intention. Your suggestion astounded them. They want to meet as soon as possible and they concur with my earlier statement. The company would take a hit financially, and thousands of jobs would be lost."

Allison paused for a moment. "Set up a meeting for me; I'll let them know my reason for getting out of the European market. We can channel our efforts elsewhere and create new jobs."

Before hanging up, David gave a tongue-in-cheek warning. "Mrs. Darlington, these men will fight to maintain their fiefdom. I hesitate to sound like an alarmist, but they may petition the court to gain control of overseas operations, claiming that you are a novice in this field."

The silence was long; Carpenter thought she had hung up. "Mrs. Darlington?" he began.

"I'm here," she replied tersely. "I have no intention of discussing this any further over the phone. Why not meet me for lunch tomorrow; by then I'll have something for you to take back to...what are their names?"

"Carl Stevenson, Brent Stokes, and Sam Greene." Carpenter rattled off the names and asked, "Where and when would you like to meet for lunch?"

"The Ritz will suffice. Meet me in the dining room at one o'clock tomorrow. Charge the meal to business expense, for the records. That suit you, Mr. Carpenter?"

"Perfectly! Till then." They disconnected.

David Carpenter rose from his recliner and glanced at his reflection in the mirror above his fireplace. He was a little flabby around the jowls, but still looked pretty good to the ladies. A twice divorced man with no intention of walking the aisle again, Carpenter was having second thoughts about bachelorhood. Allison Darlington was proving to be an interesting piece of work; had brains, was a little on the heavy side; but with all that MONEY...who cared about extra avoirdupois? He glanced once more at his mirror, gave a wink to his reflection, and began musing on how to impress a savvy lady.

David was waiting when Allison came into the dining room. He rose when she approached the table. The waiter beat him to it, pulling out her chair. Allison smiled and murmured, "Thanks, Jim." The waiter nodded, and handed each a menu.

"Coffee?"

David nodded; Allison declined and instead requested Earl Grey tea.

They drank the beverages in silence while waiting for their orders. Allison's chicken salad was delicious. David was pleased with his sirloin steak and cottage fries.

He masticated his thoughts along with the food as he waited for Allison to open the dialogue. This was her party. She nodded her head as if coming to terms with a decision.

"As George's business manager, you know he was a control freak. I lived like that at one time; now for the first time his mania for control benefits me. I contacted my former boss, and gave him an overview of my plans regarding the overseas operations to ask his advice. He got back to me this morning. Being in the stockbroker business, Mr. Baxter knows how to access information about our company's hierarchy, and I was right. I control not only the businesses stateside, but overseas investments as well. Baxter suggested rather than cause a division among our company executives, I should make a deal with them, an offer that they can't refuse. I'm going to follow his advice."

Carpenter gulped some coffee and nodded.

"I want you to inform Stevenson and the rest, that when they sell the company they're responsible for, they'll receive one third of the profit from the sale, after taxes. It's a fair and attractive proposition. Their commission is predicated on what kind of a sale they make." David's eyebrows rose a fraction, wondering how this would go over with them.

"The other option," continued Allison, "If they're loath to sell, they, themselves, will have an option to buy that property at current value, but the Darlington logo will be removed from that business." David's eyebrows rose even higher. He wouldn't bet on how that proposition would go down.

Allison handed Carpenter two documents from her huge purse. As he perused the proffered papers he groaned inwardly. He managed to smile, and remarked quietly, "I've got to hand it to you Mrs. Darlington, after reading this resume, all thoughts of taking you to court will wither like wilted flowers in a vase. No one knew anything about your background; George never admitted he had a wife, let alone one who'd been office manager in a brokerage firm." He smiled broadly and hoped she liked his smile.

Allison acknowledged his compliment with a nod. She declined the waiter's dessert menu. David followed suit. She rose from the table and held out her hand. He controlled the urge to hold it a bit longer, but she sent no vibes of interest in him. His spirits drooped.

"If there's anything further you need," he offered, "contact my office, and it will be done." He smiled down at her.

Allison thanked him, then suggested, "Let's drop the Mr. and Mrs., it gets in the way, especially if we're going to be dealing with business matters. That suit you?"

"Anything that suits you, suits me fine...Allison," he added smiling, showing his white teeth.

"Good. Let me know the outcome of my proposals to Stevenson, Greene, and Stokes." With that she bade him a good afternoon, turned, and headed for the elevators, not looking back once. He stood watching her go, marveling that she'd remembered the CEOs' names after hearing them only once. Allison looked more sophisticated than when he'd seen her earlier. Yeah, she was a good-looking dame; too rich to be single. He left the Ritz humming and thinking about conquest. Allison, on the other hand, had already dismissed David Carpenter from her mind.

CHAPTER TEN

She heard him enter the side door; felt his gaze on her back, from the kitchen doorway. Alice poured two mugs of hot java before turning to face him. She heard Mike's intake of breath.

"Holy Toledo...will the real Alice Morgan please stand up! No wonder Bert's been off his bean since your transformation."

She laughed, delighted at his compliments, and handed him a coffee mug. "Leave me out of this till I've told you why I wanted this conversation before Bert arrived." Alice sat at her desk, Mike sat across from her. He opened his mouth to speak but Alice forestalled him. "Let me say what I have to say, then I'll answer any questions you have."

He shrugged, nodded, and said, "I'm all ears."

"Mike, you know now that I was hiding here in Safe Haven from an abusive husband named George Darlington?"

Mike nodded but said nothing.

"Well, he died in a terrible car accident and his lawyer was able to reach me through my sister. I went there to bury George, pay any debts he'd left behind, then come home. But everything changed dramatically when I met with George's New York attorney. The meeting with Mr. Thornton, the lawyer, got off to a bad start. He'd bought George's tale that I'd run off with some other guy. The lawyer was cool and condescending. I finally had had enough and stood up ready to leave, but not before setting him straight about George, that he'd been cruel and twice threatened to kill me. The attorney listened, but I could see I'd not convinced him. I told him all I wanted to do was to see to George's burial, then I was returning South. I told him to keep track of the funeral expenses and I would pay for everything. It was then I saw a shift in his demeanor. He said to me,

'Mrs. Darlington, money will never be a problem. George Darlington died a very rich man.'"

Mike sat up straighter; this was getting interesting. Alice looked over at him and nodded. "When I looked surprised, Thornton asked how much I knew about George's business. I said only that he worked for a stock brokerage firm. Thornton shook his head and said he couldn't understand how a husband could keep the family's financial status from his wife. He took a huge file from a cabinet, and opened it on his desk in front of me. As he leafed through papers, he looked over at me and explained that George owned the brokerage firm and the building he worked in, plus three satellite companies as well as overseas companies. He died a multimillionaire; probably more like a billionaire.

"Mike, the shock was so great that I lost it; I broke down and began to cry. When I got hold of myself Thornton said that George had a million-dollar life insurance policy on himself; double indemnity in case of accidental death. The lawyer had already deposited most of the insurance money in a safety deposit vault for me, and put thousands in my bank account.

"I just sat in a daze. I listened as Thornton told me that George had made a new will a couple of weeks before his death. He was scheduled to sign that new will the day he died. So, the old will is still in effect, and everything George owned on earth, now belongs to me."

Mike was on his feet, but finding no place to pace, sat down again. He clapped his hand over his forehead and muttered. "This is a joke! You're pulling my leg Alice!"

Alice shook her head solemnly. "No joke Mike–that's why we're meeting. How am I going to tell Bert I'm a wealthy widow, when all he talks about is taking care of me after my disastrous marriage to George? How can he do that when I'm awash in money?" She looked at Mike for an answer. None was forthcoming.

Mike came out of deep cogitation, nodded, then winked at Alice. "This is a God thing...God removed that cretin, for if George had lived another day, someone else would have claimed the booty. Bert can't fault God for raining green manna from heaven; especially when he and I've been praying for the stuff so we can keep our church doors oiled."

Mike stopped and walked over to replenish his coffee mug. "Alice... not to worry. Our man of the cloth has brains. Yes, he wants to take care of you, but he's not about to let you go because you've GOT moola. His pride'll take a beating, but he'll get over his pique." Mike threw back his head and roared with laughter. "Boy oh boy...the other night when we prayed for help; who'd have thought God was going to rain down buckets full of green stuff? Play your cards right Alice, my girl. Look pained when he looks distressed; lament that you'll need him more now than ever. You're a defenseless rich minnow surrounded by hungry sharks." Mike stood and hugged her. "Hey I gotta go, I have a client coming at 9 a.m. No Aunt Susie in my ancestral tree about to cross over and leave me her loot." He laughed and was gone.

Alice looked at her watch; half an hour and Bert would be in his office. She'd not phoned the night before, he didn't know she was home. She made fresh coffee and set Danish rolls on a plate, closed the kitchen door, and waited his arrival.

What a night of tossing and turning he'd had. Why hadn't Alice called? Nagging fears; maybe someone from the past cropped up. He couldn't rid himself of jealousy. Their relationship was still fragile. He was behind normal schedule when he sat down behind his desk to prioritize a pile of pink slips from the day before. He sighed at the size of the pile. A discreet knock on the door; "Come in Ruthie," he answered, and returned to perusing the slips. "You've been busy drumming up people for me to call," he said mournfully.

No answer; a tray was slid on the far end of his desk. Looking up, he gasped, jumped to his feet, and rushed around the desk. Alice was in his arms. "Alice, honey, when'd you get home?" She nestled against his chest, while he kissed the top of her hair rocking her and crooning, "Honey, honey, I'm so glad you're back safely in my arms."

They stood locked in embrace, but Alice didn't raise her face for his eager kisses. She pushed him gently away and said quietly, "Pastor, let's have coffee; we need to talk." Her voice was calm but definite. Bert backed away, confused by this new formality. He sat down heavily in his chair, but didn't swivel. Alarm bells clanged in his ears, his body, inert. His nighttime fears surfaced. Alice was going to dump him, return to New York where she belonged. His brow was wet, his armpits seeping like a fountain, staining his shirt. What a mess.

He watched Alice pour coffee into two china mugs he'd never seen before, from a new carafe. He watched as she pushed a plate of his favorite strawberry tarts near him. How can she be so calm, do such mundane things while I'm sitting here going to pieces? Have I ever meant anything to her? She's so different, and so lovely, he mused longingly. And I'm a nothing.

Alice didn't look his way until she finished her ministrations. Bert said a small grace, and reached for a coffee mug. He lifted the brew to his mouth, but couldn't drink. Alice sipped hers and smiled a tentative smile.

Oh God, he prayed silently, what am I going to do if she leaves me? The room was so quiet. He waited for her to speak; she just sipped coffee. Unable to bear the silence any longer, Bert spoke, quietly, heart in his mouth. "If you're going to tell me you've changed your mind about us, just come out with it, at least relieve the misery of not knowing." His voice trembled. He was near tears, afraid to drink coffee lest he choked.

"No, no, Bert," she said softly. "I haven't changed my mind about you, but something's come up that could change your mind about wanting me."

"Alice!" he exclaimed, starting to rise from his chair.

But Alice shook her head and continued, "Please, Bert, you need to hear me out."

He sat down and picked up his coffee cup and for the first time drank thirstily. "Alice, you're the woman I love. I don't care what you've got to say. I want to marry you! Whatever mess your ex got you into is of no consequence. I love you and want to take care of you. Now let's hear what this is all about, because it nearly caused me to have a coronary from worry." He sipped more coffee and gazed at her lovingly.

Alice smiled and began. "You remember when I left for New York, I had no idea what I'd find regarding George's financial status. I went to see that he had a decent burial, and pay any debts he owed." She looked over at him and Bert nodded.

"Yes I remember and I give you credit for being so decent about doing the right thing."

Alice shrugged. "Well, hiding from him didn't change the fact that I was still his wife. George's attorney, Albert Thornton, arranged to see me as soon as I got to New York. I visited him in his office on Tuesday. He was politeness incased in ice; proper yet condescending. I figured he believed the tales George had spun about me. Well, I finally had enough and rose to leave. He panicked and coaxed me to remain. I said I would but I needed to put matters straight regarding George. I told him just what kind of a sadist George was, and why I ran. I knew by his looks he was skeptical of my story. I finally told him to keep track of the cost of the funeral; I'd asked his office to take care of it, and any debts George left behind, I was prepared to pay.

"It was then that his demeanor changed, his body relaxed and his voice lost its edge. He asked how much I knew about my husband's business affairs. I said, nothing! Only that he worked for a stockbroker firm, and seemed to be successful. George never discussed his work with me.

"Thornton tisked, tisked, and went to a file cabinet and came back with a bulging folder. He said, 'Mrs. Darlington, you've been robbed of information due you as his wife. George Darlington did not work for any firm, George Darlington owned the firm and three subsidiaries in other states, as well as overseas investments. Your late husband died a multimillionaire.'"

Bert didn't move a muscle. Was Alice fantasizing? Surely this couldn't be true?

"Bert, I don't know why, but I started crying. I'd been nothing to George but a punching bag and a dogsbody doing his bidding. Cut off from even the mundane that exists between spouses...like talking about financial matters...everything was kept from me. I felt so low."

Bert longed to take her in his arms, let her cry out her humiliation, but now wasn't the time. Questions were surfacing, but as a counselor, he kept quiet till she finished.

Alice paused and looked over at him. "Thornton told me that two weeks before George's death, he'd made a new will. He was scheduled to come to Thornton's office the day he was killed. The new will was never signed. The old will still stands." She blew her nose and wiped her eyes.

Bert stretched his arms across the desk in her direction. "With the new will unsigned..." he let the sentence peter out. He couldn't ask, but watched her fold and unfold a paper napkin before looking his way. She gave a little deprecating shrug and a faint smile.

"Everything George Darlington owned in this world belongs to me. I'm sole beneficiary." She hadn't known what to expect from Bert. He sat there staring into space, mouth half open but no words coming out.

Alice, drained emotionally after reciting her story twice in one morning, felt anger and resentment creep into the situation. Now was the time she needed his arms around her, not him sitting like some zombie trying to figure things out. She needed him NOW. She gathered her cup, rose from her chair, and left the office.

Bert, drowning in contradictory pros and cons, was oblivious of her departure. The ringing of a phone, followed by muffled conversation, had him running to Alice's office.

Alice was speaking softly to the person on the other end; her back was toward him. Bert slipped his arms around her and drew her to him. She stiffened. He held her all the tighter and whispered, "Please give a guy a little slack. It's not every day you get hit with news like that. I'm still reeling from it." She said nothing, but he felt her relax.

"I'll have Pastor get back to you, Molly, before the day's out. And don't worry; I'm sure this is just a phase she's going through. Yes, I will. Talk to you later." She hung up the phone.

Without hesitating, Bert turned her around and planted a serious kiss on her lips. Alice sighed, and leaned closer to him. "That's more like it," he said, kissing the top of her head.

"We've got lots to talk about but let me say this before we begin. You're my woman and I am going to marry you, if you'd inherited Fort Knox. Now, I've some unfinished business to take care of in the office. Come along–you're needed in this." Alice sat down while Bert rummaged through his desk, came up with something he hid behind his back, and approached her. Bert knelt on one knee clumsily and opened the little box. Alice gasped. It was a beautiful diamond solitaire with two diamonds on each side of the band.

"Alice," he said huskily. "I love you with all my heart, soul and body... please honey will you do me the honor of marrying me?" The tears pooling in her eyes let go and cascaded down her cheeks as she nodded her acceptance. He slipped the ring on her ring finger and pulled her into his arms. "Alice, Alice...how I've longed for this moment. You'll never, never regret marrying this poor preacher. Heaven sent you to me, and I'll never leave you, till death takes me home." Bert was having difficulty keeping tears from running down his cheeks. He kissed her long and hard, and she returned his kisses in kind. Allison Evans Darlington had never known love before. God was good. He had given her the man of her dreams...at last.

"Honey," said Bert coming up for air. "Can we keep your inheritance a secret, you know...not publish the fact that I'm marrying you for your money?" he teased.

"Good grief, Bert, can you imagine the lines that would form around our church if word got out about this inheritance? On my way home from New York an idea flashed across my mind. It's still too ethereal to put into words, but when it's clearer I'll let you know what I believe God wants us to do with George's money." He looked at her inquiringly. Bert was about to say something, when she put up her hand. "Humor me, honey. I'll fill you in when I've got things straight in my mind, OK?" He shrugged and bent to kiss her, intrigued by the twinkle in her eye.

CHAPTER ELEVEN

De ja vu, thought Bert, drinking Molly Brown's tantalizing coffee in a cracked mug. Ed, in sweat pants and an old sweater, sat moodily, waiting for Pastor to solve the problem they'd called him about. Molly hovered over the kitchen table, coffee pot in hand, trying to look relaxed and failing miserably. The Browns picked up their ears when Bert asked, "How long's Lisa been acting up?" Ed looked at Molly for specifics.

"Well, I haven't really kept track, Pastor, but the nearest I can come up with is, maybe a little over a month." Ed nodded in agreement.

"What change did you notice...you know...was there anything Lisa said or did to raise a red flag in your head?"

Molly thought; Ed answered. "Yeah, she announced one night after the kids had gone to bed that she was changing churches. She'd visited this church where her friends were all going one Sunday night, and said she really liked it, that it was full of young people. She said that since she's almost 17, she wants to try something different, that our church is OK for us, but she wants to be able to hang out with other teens. She wants more than a sermon out of the Bible from church; she prefers loud music and lots of emotion."

"Lisa home now?" asked Bert. The Browns looked embarrassed.

"She left when she knew you were coming," said her dad.

"She's supposed to be doing homework with a friend," added Molly, lamely. "But she's not staying out late or anything like that."

"What did you say when she gave her ultimatum regarding church attendance?" asked Bert.

Molly looked over at Ed, who shrugged and said bluntly, "I told her no way was she leaving the church she'd been brought up in, saved and baptized in. Christians didn't go to church to get entertained. They went to church to worship God and get strength and guidance for their lives. Some guys at work say their kids go to this church called Awakening; they say it's rock and roll, strobe lights, dry ice to create some kind of mysticism, lots of swaying with arms extended, eyes closed. The guys say they'd never seen anything like it in a church service before. Full of jumping, dancing kids, loving it.

"Preacher, I feel dirty talkin' about 'em when I hear that lots of souls are being saved...." Ed trailed off; Bert refrained from making any comment on that observation...it was a conundrum.

"So," Bert got back to the subject, "Lisa's been attending Awakening?" They nodded miserably.

"What could I do preacher, when she left the house Sunday morning, with a piece of toast, car keys in hand, and just drove off? We were home from church when she came home. So help me, she had a satisfied smirk on her face. I had an urge to slap it...but of course, I didn't. She set the pattern that morning; we've been chewing her out ever since. Lisa says we can't stop her from choosing her place of worship. She's got a point there. And Bert, I understand to a certain point her wanting to be with her peers. If her persona hadn't changed for the worse, we wouldn't be so upset. But she's become an arrogant, rude girl; impatient with her siblings. Ignores her mother's instructions and hardly speaks to me. She's not the Lisa of a few months ago." Ed turned and faced Bert. "So that's why we called you. You've counseled lots of people; what do you suggest we do with our Lisa?"

Molly topped Bert's cup, perhaps unconsciously hoping additional caffeine would spur his thinking and produce a miraculous solution. Bert nodded his thanks, drank slowly, and looked across the table where they sat in anticipation. "I have a suggestion, but it'll only work if you both agree to it. Other than that, it's a waste of time trying."

In unison they practically shouted, "Oh we will...we're desperate. We'll work together." Their eagerness was palpable; he felt sorry for them.

"When Lisa comes home tonight, Ed, ask to see her car keys." He looked at Ed, who nodded. Molly gave a little gasp; Bert knew she'd divined his suggestion. She kept quiet, but fear was on her face. "Now," said Bert. "Tell her she'll get her car keys back when her attitude toward members of the family is back to where it was months ago. Say nothing about church. Forcing her back to our church is not what we want. I don't want our church held up as a pawn. We come to church to worship God, not because if we don't, we'll be deprived of some cherished possession."

"But preacher, how would she get to school?" whispered Molly.

"How did she get to school before she got her car? She's had it how long?" asked Bert.

"She rode the school bus," Ed put in, "till we got her the car six months ago."

"She can reacquaint herself with the school bus," said the preacher.

Molly was tearing a paper napkin into shreds. Her eyes flitted to Ed and then to Bert. "She'd be so unhappy," said Lisa's mother. "She loves that car."

Bert shrugged. "If you're wanting a solution without pain, I've none to offer, Molly. You take steps to rectify the situation now, or leave it alone and see it worsen the older she gets."

"She'll put up a fuss," said her dad. "She's developed quite a temper."

"I'm coming to that," said Bert. "If she goes ballistic, and she probably will, tell her if her attitude worsens, you'll stop monthly payments on her cell phone. That threat will get her attention. Kids walk around with cells glued to their ears these days, as if it's a compass."

They sat in silence till Bert looked at his watch, and started to rise. "Preacher, don't go," said Molly. "I know you're right...something big has to happen or Lisa'll never change her attitude. But will she hate us for doing this to her?" Molly began to cry. Ed looked grim but said nothing.

"Of course she will," said the preacher. "So would any of us at that age. But remember the fifth commandment, 'Honor thy father and thy mother.' It's an important commandment, for God added a blessing of longevity to those who honor parents. I could make a case for you that by not stopping her unruly behavior, you are enabling her to break that commandment. But the bottom line is this: You are concerned about her changed character. Right?" They nodded. "Isn't that worth trying tough love to save her from grief down the road?" They looked at each other and nodded.

"We'll do it Pastor. Molly'll be OK once she gets her mind round to what's good for Lisa. And I'm anxious to put an end to this division."

Ed walked Bert to the front door, opened it; put on the porch light and waited till Bert was in his car. He watched the preacher drive slowly out of the driveway, then turned to Molly.

"You gotta help me, honey. I'm scared to death Lisa'll run away." Molly Brown put her arms around his waist and leaned into him.

"We gotta try, like Bert said...for Lisa's sake."

He called as soon as he got home. "You OK honey? Wish it weren't so late; I'd love to see you before I turn in."

"Bert, I just got off the phone with my real estate agent. The buyer's wanting to close on my house this week; wants to buy some of my furnishings. So it looks like back to New York I go. I'll probably go early Thursday morning, and be back the following Tuesday." She heard him sigh. "I know dear, I know; I hate it as much as you do, but what option do I have? Incidentally how did your visit with the Browns turn out?"

"Well, they were reluctant to follow my advice, but agreed something had to be done. We'll see. I gave them the advice we talked about this afternoon. Molly was afraid it would inconvenience Lisa...just like a mother. Willing to suffer abuse rather than give the kid any pain. But they may surprise me. Ed seemed pretty sold on it; Molly's more of a pushover where Lisa's concerned."

"Mmhmm," murmured Alice, and changed the subject. "I'll take care of the refreshments for our engagement party before I leave for New York. How are you going to announce it?"

Bert started to laugh. "You kidding? I'm gonna have Ruth put an announcement in Sunday's bulletin stating that at Wednesday night's prayer meeting, the preacher is going to introduce his significant other." He laughed when he heard her shriek.

"You wouldn't!"

"Sure I would...and will. It's no lie, and that's the vernacular used today when describing someone special, their significant other." Bert was laughing, then in a sober tone added, "It'll upset those who were hoping any special announcement would be my resignation. As much as I hate to see you leave, it's probably just as well that you're not seen around town till the day of unveiling." He laughed, and Alice felt better about leaving him–again.

Before heading back to New York, Alice made arrangements with the local catering company and the florist for the engagement celebration that they'd discussed after the ring was on her finger. She ordered a huge two-tier slab cake from the bakery.

"Prepare for 200 guests," she advised the caterer. "I want your finest finger food; don't worry about the cost. Use real china, cutlery; tablecloths and cloth napkins. And, fix goodie bags for every guest to take home." The florist was assigned the job of decorating the fellowship hall. Simple but elegant, she told her.

Lisa Brown was home a couple of hours after the preacher left. She was at the refrigerator when Ed came into the kitchen.

"Let me see your car keys, Lisa," he said calmly. Lisa took them from her purse that lay on the kitchen table, and held them up. He took them from her, put them in his pocket, and said, "You'll get them back when your attitude toward your family has changed for the better." Ed turned and started toward his bedroom. Lisa was speechless.

"DAD!" she screamed. "Dad, you can't do that! It's MY car. How am I going to get to school in the morning?" She yelled down the hall, "Mom, Mom! Do you know what Dad just did? He took my car keys! Mom, make him give them back to me. MOM!"

Molly came out of the bedroom and stood beside Ed. She was trembling but her voice was calm. "You heard your father; we've had enough of your insulting behavior. It's up to you when you get your keys back."

"But...but...how am I gonna get to school in the morning?!"

"The school bus still runs," said Molly and went back to their bedroom, Ed following, closing the door.

Lisa stood at their door and pounded on it. "I'm going to tell my school counselor, she'll turn you in to social services for depriving me of school transportation. I hate you...hear? I hate you." She began crying and pounding their door.

Ed opened it, stood looking at his distraught daughter, and said firmly, "Lisa, if you pull any social service stuff on me, I will sell that car and you will never get another car from me. And furthermore, if you don't behave yourself in the meantime, I'll cancel your cell contract."

Lisa went white. "You wouldn't dare!"

"Try me," said Ed Brown, shutting the door.

By the next morning, Lisa had resigned herself to riding the school bus, seething with rage at her parents. Ed was at work, the younger kids already riding their school bus. Before leaving the house, Lisa took her anger out on Molly. "Dad's nothing but a low life...works at a crummy lumber mill 'cause he didn't even finish high school. He's never tried to better himself like other girls' dads have."

Molly Brown, bristling with disgust, turned furiously on her and shouted, "How dare you! How dare you say such things about the father who's working overtime to pay for the car you drive and that cell phone you never have off your ear. Your attitude changed along with your values when you switched friends and started hanging around with Cindy Hunt and her gang. We're not in their league, nor do we want their values. They're the people who are trying to get rid of our pastor. Now get to school. And if I ever hear you speak that way about your dad again I'll slap your mouth, and dare you to call social services. And I'll insist that your dad gets rid of your car. Now get out of my sight, you disgust me."

This was the longest and most virulent speech Lisa had ever heard from Molly's mouth. She knew she'd gone too far and wondered how she could have said those things about her dad. Lisa Brown closed the front door quietly and headed for the bus stop. She sat at the back, making eye contact with no one, and buried her face behind a book.

Cindy Hunt and two classmates drove into the parking lot as the school bus disgorged its passengers. Lisa was descending from the bus as Cindy drove by. She hoped they hadn't seen her exit the bus. In the hall, Cindy caught up with her. "Slumming this morning, Lisa?"

Lisa wanted to lie, but saw no point in it. She shrugged. "I'm being punished. Dad took my wheels. When I'm a good girl again, I'll get 'em back." She tried to joke it away, but it had its consequence.

"Boy," said Cindy, "if my old man pulled a trick like that on me, I'd call social services, maybe even leave home."

"Me too!" chorused Penny Akins and Judy Stevens, as the girls walked ahead of but not with Lisa, a snub she recognized. Body language was a language she was too familiar with, having met it often enough when she was outside the clique. Now she sensed she was on the verge of being shunned by the privileged few. Emptiness was added to her misery.

Days of stalemate followed the car episode. Lisa rode the bus, and after her dinner chores, she retired to her bedroom, to her cell and her homework. Ed and Molly missed her company but as Ed said, "Better her in her room than ranting in the kitchen."

Sunday morning Ed and his family left for church; Lisa stayed put in her room till she heard them drive off, then went to the kitchen to eat cold cereal. Time with nothing to use it on ratcheted up her misery. Not one of her friends had offered to pick her up for church. She hinted to Cindy that she needed a ride. Cindy shrugged it off. "Surely you've got someone who'll do that for you," she retorted, but didn't offer to be that someone.

Lisa channel-surfed for a religious program, but after flipping through one station after another, she turned the TV off and went into her bedroom, frustrated and miserable.

"What am I doing?" Lisa cried aloud. "I'm miserable. I never used to be miserable." Tears coursed down her cheeks and continued till her cries all but choked her.

She opened up her Bible and a devotional book that had gone long untouched at her bedside. The words of the page of the devotional spoke to her deeply: "Christians can't just change hats and be comfortable in a new chapeau. We're to emulate Christ's values, not values of the world. It goes against our inner self and we're miserable trying to be someone we're not."

She thought about her attitude toward her parents lately, and how different it was from her previous respectful treatment of them. Her heart was saddened as the realization of her sin hit her square in the face. "Oh God, what have I done?" she prayed. "Please forgive me, Lord, and give me the courage to make things right with my family."

Lisa wiped her tears away, and knew what she needed to do. She went to the dining room and set the table for dinner, pouring water into glasses and straightening up the kitchen. She was checking to see if Molly's roast was progressing when the family arrived home from church. Molly, as usual, headed immediately to the kitchen to check on the roast. Her eyes widened when she saw the table set, the kitchen clean, and Lisa standing with a hopeful look on her face.

Lisa gave her mom a sheepish grin as if being caught doing something wrong. Molly crossed to Lisa, and folded her in her arms murmuring, "Oh honey, so good to have you back."

Lisa nodded, and said tearfully, "Yeah, mom, the prodigal's back, and the fatted calf's in the oven."

Ed had difficulty saying grace, but he got through it and finished with, "And God, thanks for returning our Lisa to us."

When the family was otherwise occupied, Ed made a call to Bert. "Pastor, pastor! Our Lisa's back to her cheerful self. Praise the Lord, praise the Lord!"

Bert smiled on the other end of the line, looking up to heaven and said, "Thank you, God."

CHAPTER TWELVE

Fair Haven Baptist Church, in all its 54 years, had never witnessed such a Wednesday night prayer meeting. Alice's intuition that they'd have a least 200 members show up, was right on the money. Excitement was palpable. At 6:15 the curtain was up and Sylvia leaned heavily on the piano keys. Mike, smartly turned out thanks to Ruth, beamed as he stood looking out at the congregation. While Mike had their attention, Alice slipped in beside Ruth to the second-row pew to Bert's right. She kept her head down, interacting only with Ruth and her children.

"I must say," began Mike, tongue in cheek, "that I've never known you all to be in such need of prayer as you are tonight. And perish the thought that you should be here for anything but praying for your souls." Laughter, laughter. "Whatever...it's great to see your smiling faces. And believe me, before this night's over you'll have plenty to smile about. Now let's lift our voices to God and sing 'Love Lifted Me,' page 34 in your hymnals, or follow the dancing ball on the screen." Laughter.

The mood was genial, and the people sang with enthusiasm and happiness. At 6:40 Bert made his entrance via the choir door. The singing all but stopped when he stepped onto the platform. Who could sing and gape at the same time, when their pastor, all gussied up in an elegant gray jacket over lighter gray slacks, made his way to the pulpit? His white shirt was sporting a tie that hadn't been bought in Safe Haven. Men near enough to see Bert's shoes recognized them as custom-made. Pastor Davenport had never looked happier.

"C'mon folk," moaned Mike. "Don't leave me singing a solo." The congregation found its place and returned to singing with renewed verve.

Without prompting and to the amazement of others, Joe Elliot stood up and began clapping. Sensing the reason, others in the congregation rose to their feet and directed their applause to Bert, clapping loudly. Joe shouted, "Preacher you look like a bridegroom." Laughter was followed by more applause, while an astonished Bert beamed appreciatively at his flock.

The applause lasted till Bert repeated his thanks over and over again, then asked the congregation to be seated. "We've got a lot to do this evening. Mike, we'll disappoint John Folk tonight, and skip the offering. Could you please pray for tonight's service?"

Mike complied. When the prayer was over, Mike sat down on the front row pew to Bert's left, beaming happily.

Bert looked at his people and loved them, though some were easier to love than others. They were the sheep of his pasture that he was ordained to feed the Word of God, not the word of the world. He had to restrain himself from looking at Alice; he wanted to send her a message of love but knew he couldn't look at her yet. Bert saluted his congregation with a raised water glass and said, "Well, before I tickle your ears with my announcement, let me direct your attention to First Corinthians, chapter thirteen." A few groans emitted from the crowd. Bert laughed. "C'mon folk. You'd be disappointed if I didn't read something from the Good Book before you went home. I promise this is a very, very short sermon. It's about LOVE and coincidental to my announcement tonight."

Pages rustled and solemnity descended as Bert read Paul's beautiful words. "Though I speak with the tongues of men and of angels and have not love, I am become as sounding brass or a tinkling cymbal...and though I bestow all my goods to feed the poor, and though I give my body to be burned, and have not love, it profits me nothing." Bert heard some quiet amens and knew his people were in tune with his mood.

"Paul couldn't have penned these soul-revealing words without help from God. God IS love, or charity. Before meeting Christ, Paul hated Jesus. When he met the Master, he was never the same. The transformed Paul became the greatest and most prolific writer of the New Testament. In this chapter he delineates love's characteristics dictated from the Divine, Himself. Love suffers long, is kind, doesn't behave unseemly, is not boastful, does not envy. Love is not puffed up, not easily provoked, does not entertain evil thoughts. Love rejoices in the truth; bears all things, believes all things, hopes all things, endures all things. Who of us can say we have kept the laws of love God gave Paul, to pass to the Corinthians and eventually to us?" Bert took a sip of water before finishing. "Life is temporal, tongues cease, prophecies fail, knowledge vanishes away. But love, like God, is eternal. The chapter ends with the memorable words: "And now abides faith, hope, charity, these three; but the greatest of these is charity–love!"

Bert closed his Bible, took off his glasses, and wiped his eyes. No one stirred; coughs took a holiday. "I called this meeting tonight to introduce you to the woman God sent my way." Feet shuffled, bodies bent forward; no one wanted to miss a word.

"The woman I'd fallen in love with was out of my reach; for although she'd been estranged from her husband for years, she still had a husband. I couldn't tell her how I felt. Duty forbade that I woo another man's wife. A few weeks ago that all changed; the husband was killed in a car accident. Freed from the bond that held her, I was able to pursue her and believe you me this is one time I didn't procrastinate." Laughter and applause.

"Good for you preacher!" said a male voice in the back.

"The night some of you saw me kissing her in Charlie's parking lot was the night she said she'd consider taking me on." Laughter, applause.

"She is no stranger to you; she has worked among you for seven years. You will not recognize her. She's been hiding from an abusive man who threatened twice to kill her. She has come out of the shadows and is the person she once was before her unfortunate ordeal. Now folks I'd like you to meet the woman I love; the woman who is wearing my ring, and the woman I want to marry as soon as possible." People craned their necks trying to see who Bert was looking at.

"Alice, honey, come on up and let your family greet you." Silence. Someone whispered loudly, "Alice? Surely not his secretary!"

A gasp went through the assembly when Alice rose and approached the platform. Bert was there with his hand extended as she climbed the three steps to stand beside him. She was lovely in her soft mauve dress, her blonde head coiffed to perfection. The overhead lights caught the brilliance of her diamond earrings and pendant; prisms of colors danced above their heads. Bert's arms were around her. She was blushing happily, and smiling at the congregation. Not a peep was heard; the members were in shock.

Bert held up her left hand for all to see the diamond on her third finger. "I'm hoping she won't keep me waiting long." Bert turned her around and kissed her.

Sylvia let loose on the keyboard with, "Let Me Call You Sweetheart." The congregation woke from its daze and joined in heartily. It had been some time since the people had been of one spirit, loving and caring for the church. Eyes wept and throats cleared, as they remembered their own heady days of new love and commitment. Love is the greatest gift God bestowed on man. Without love we are nothing!

Mike brought sanity to the moment by announcing, "Pastor and Alice invite you to their engagement celebration in the fellowship hall. Please wait for the usher to come to your pew, that way, there will be no pushing or shoving. You parents, please corral your kids...keep them beside you. I'm going to do the same with my three young 'uns. Now let's pray for God's blessing on the food of this wonderful occasion."

Alice and Bert left the auditorium first. Sylvia played "I Want a Girl Just Like the Girl That Married Dear Old Dad" while the audience followed Mike's instructions for exiting, and headed to the fellowship hall.

Bert and Alice stood under a bower of fresh flowers, next to the table bearing the beautifully decorated cake bearing their names entwined in hearts and rings. The members gasped at the transformed hall. Mood music played softly in the background. Their pastor had never looked happier or younger. Alice, face flushed and smiling, greeted the members and thanked them for coming, and for the compliments they heaped on her.

Eight tables laden with identical food were spaced strategically around the hall. A large refreshment table held every kind of soft drink, tea and coffee. Waiters and waitresses were at the ready to help the guests.

Choruses of exclamations floated around the room: "Never saw the place look like this before." "Boy, this musta cost a bundle; who's paying for all this?" "Who cares, eat and enjoy." "Can't be the church; John Folk's over there all smiles." Laughter. "Yeah, he'd be glowering if he had to reach into the church purse to pay for this." Laughter. "Alice is beautiful; can you imagine hiding all those years behind that ugly hairdo and horrible glasses?" "Pastor's in love–and it's about time, he's been single long enough." "Think they'll drop their push to get rid of Bert, now that he's about to get married?" "I'll wager they haven't a clue as to what they're up against with Alice in the picture." Laughter, laughter. "Alice is no pushover. And she's in love with our preacher...even a blind man can spot that."

It was well after ten when Bert drove Alice to her apartment. The doorman opened the car door for Alice. "Don't bother seeing me to the door, Bert...just go home. I know you're as beat as I am."

He looked at her gratefully and nodded. He leaned over and kissed her. "Honey," he admitted, "I've never been happier, nor more tired."

Alice laughed. "We'll talk in the morning dear. Goodnight."

Greg Hunt had elected to stay home, but Madeline and ten-year-old Greg, Jr. attended the surprise celebration. "Daddy," shouted Junior, bursting into the family room where Greg lay sprawled out on his recliner. "You shoulda been there; wow! what a party. Best food I've ever eaten in the fellowship hall. And look what they gave everyone when we left." He held up a box inside a bright cellophane bag. "Full of goodies!"

"Go to bed," growled his dad.

"Yes, off to bed with you son, this is a school night. And put that bag in the fridge; you've had enough to eat tonight." Madeline put her hands on his shoulders and gently nudged him in the proper direction.

Greg sat up straight in his chair. "What's this all about a party...tonight at church?"

Madeline nodded. "An engagement party. Preacher introduced us to his mystery lady. The congregation went wild. I don't know when I've enjoyed myself as much as I did tonight. The place was packed. Probably over 200. I wish you would have been there, Greg, you missed the event of a lifetime. We met the future Mrs. Davenport, and you'll never guess who she is."

Greg feigned indifference, wanted to quip "Frankly my dear, I don't give a damn..." but refrained. He waited impatiently for his wife to give him the name of the bride-to-be. But Madeline was side-tracked and already talking about something else. "Well?" he finally said peevishly. "Are you going to tell me who the lucky dame is, or do we play twenty questions?"

Madeline laughed. "Sorry. But you'll never believe that his future bride is Alice Morgan."

Greg popped the button on his recliner and sat upright. Clapping his hand to his forehead he exclaimed, "That bag lady! Good grief, is she the best our broken-down preacher could catch?"

Madeline let out peals of laughter. "Wait till you see her! She's fantastic; groomed to the nines, wearing jewelry that cost a fortune. She's one sophisticated lady. I'd be willing to bet her outfit cost more than I spend all year on my clothes. Looks like she's no stranger where money's concerned. I'd say our preacher's marrying UP!" Madeline smirked as consternation passed over Greg's face. "Yeah, now you boys will have Alice to deal with when you try ousting her man from his perch. She comes across as one savvy lady who can fight for the man she loves." Madeline was tired of Greg and the others trying to oust Bert. She liked the pastor, and hated being in the middle, caught between loyalty to Greg and pulling for the preacher.

Greg left her talking and went to his office, closing the door and grabbing his cell. "Jay, you go to church tonight?" He listened as Jay Butler waxed enthusiastically over the reception.

"Big money spent on that party, let me tell you," came the reply.

Greg's frown deepened, sweat gathering at his hairline. "Yeah, so Madeline said. Church pick up the tab?"

"Nope. John Folk was all smiles, eating that great food like the rest of us, and enjoying it."

"Then who picked up the tab?" demanded Greg.

Jay at the other end replied, "Hey, Greg, I dunno...I sure didn't, but it was the best food we've eaten in that hall."

Before disconnecting, Greg said firmly, "We need to meet before the church forgets Faulkner's message, and gets chummy with the future Mrs. Davenport. Call the guys. Set it up here for Friday night at 8:00. OK? See you then." He hung up before Jay Butler had a chance to answer.

Bert's landline rang as he was leaving for the office. Annoyed, he reached for the ringing instrument. "Yes, this..."

"Well you old dog! Didn't know you were chasing skirts at your age." Laughter followed protracted silence. Bert grinned when he finally recognized the North Carolina number on his caller ID.

"How on earth did you find out so soon?" demanded Bert.

"Now padre, don't tell me you've forgotten the lightning speed church gossip travels. And to further expedite tittle-tattle, remember one of my sheep is cousin to one of your lambs. She dutifully keeps us informed of the scandals going on in your pen." Dr. Ivo Hinton stopped pulling Bert's chain to remark, "I called to congratulate you and the bride to be. Do I know her? Have I met her?"

"You might have seen Alice in the office when you visited. She's been my secretary. She came from New York around the time Jenny had to quit working."

"Hmmm," murmured Hinton. "Only person I remember of your office staff was an old woman with an awful hairdo, with not a smidgen of sex appeal."

Bert started laughing and couldn't stop. "What'd I say that was so outlandishly funny?" demanded Hinton.

"You just described my bride to be," confessed Bert. "Only you saw her in camouflage mode. Wouldn't recognize her now!"

Dr. Hinton held his tongue, but his eyebrows rose an inch. He shook his head and remarked, "Well, I'll take your word for it; when's the wedding?"

"Dunno. Alice's husband died a few weeks ago, but she's been estranged from him for seven years. A real bastard. Fill you in later on that score. But I'm ready when she gives the word."

"When are you due for a Sabbatical?"

"Anytime. Didn't take my last one; Jenny was too sick."

"Well then, you've got time coming. Shouldn't be hard to convince your lady love that your Sabbatical would be ideal for your nuptials. Planning on a church wedding?"

Bert groaned. "At this stage in life, I'd just as soon slip away, marry quietly. But it'll be Alice's call."

"Well," said indefatigable Dr. Ivo Hinton, "if all other preachers turn you down as being too immature for marriage," Hinton chuckled, "I just might be persuaded to tie the knot. I can tie knots in my sleep these days."

His laugh was infectious. "And, Bert, we've a lovely Mary/Martha wedding chapel to boot."

Bert said dolefully, "I'll remember your willingness to put your reputation on the line to help a fellow pastor." Changing his tone, he remarked, "That wedding chapel sounds exactly what I'd like to use. If Alice is amenable, we'll take you up on your offer. Thanks Ivo, I'll get back to you when I have something to tell you. God bless."

Bert wasted no time passing on Hinton's suggestion to Alice. He picked up the phone and relayed the information to his beloved. "See honey, I can take my Sabbatical, we can drive to North Carolina and get married in this lovely chapel. Ivo Hinton will perform the ceremony. Think about it dearest, and let me know and I'll make arrangements with Hinton."

"It sounds perfect Bert. It'll relieve me of having to plan a wedding, especially with all I've got facing me in New York. I need to tag the items I'm sending here and let the realtor take over selling the things I'm not keeping. And, after our engagement party, I'm all played out. But I don't want a repeat of that ghastly Las Vegas elopement."

"Alice, Alice, honey. I'd never subject you to such humiliation. No, this chapel is beautiful; white interior, red plush pews and carpeting, organ, the whole works. A bride's dream, or so I'm told. But you can see for yourself on the Internet. Think it over and get back with me. I'll let Hinton know; he's anxious to perform the ceremony. You'll like him, he's quite a guy."

After sweet nothings passed between them, they disconnected.

"God is so good; God is so..." Bert stopped singing. What was John Folk's car doing at church on a weekday morning? Something's up! In the 18 years he'd known him, Folk had never deviated from his fixed routine. He was at his insurance office every morning tending to business; anything church related was handled in the evening. As Bert entered the side door, he heard laughter. Well, he thought, at least Folk isn't here because of some calamity.

John was leaning against the doorpost of Alice's office talking to Ruth. He heard Bert and moved to meet him. "Got something to show you Bert," said John, taking Bert's elbow and piloting him to his office.

Bert barely had a chance to greet Ruth with, "Good morning... anything new?" She shook her head and pointed toward his desk where several messages lay waiting.

As soon as he was seated, Bert said, "OK, let's hear what's got you in a twist."

John closed the door quietly, sat across from Bert's desk and to an astonished Bert, began clapping his hands gleefully. Folk stopped laughing long enough to extricate a business envelope from his inner jacket pocket and slide it over to Bert. Bert looked quizzically first at John, then at the envelope.

"What's this all about John?" he asked cautiously.

John chortled. "You know Bert, you're always preaching about miracles." Bert nodded. "Well," continued John, "I've always been a little skeptical about miracles happening in the 21st century. But you see sitting before you a man totally convinced that miracles still happen, converted by the contents of that letter."

He pointed to the letter in front of Bert. "It appeared in my post office box this morning. Read it preacher! Read it, and tell me if this isn't a modern-day miracle."

Bert slid the letter from the envelope and read it once, then twice. "The enclosed check for $50,000 is a gift to Fair Haven Baptist Church, to be used for structural improvements of the building. The Rev. Robert Davenport is fully authorized to spend the money on projects he deems important to the church property. The donor proffers this gift because of Rev. Davenport's dedication to preaching the gospel of salvation in the face of changing cultural views. The donor prefers anonymity, preferring the blessings of God rather than plaudits of men. God bless."

Bert lingered over the letter, afraid to look up lest John divine that Bert knew who the donor was. John Folk had a reputation for being fey, something handed down to him from a Scottish ancestor blessed or cursed with the ability to see into men's minds. Finally, shaking his head incredulously, he asked John, "You've made sure this isn't some gimmick, I suppose?"

"Of course, of course. You don't think I'd not check it out before bringing it here? It's the real deal," he chortled. "I was at the bank as soon as it opened and talked with the bank manager. The money's good but information about the donor is blocked." He shrugged. "Let the guy have his anonymity. We've got live cash. When I deposit this check, it'll be the first time in church history our account has entertained such a royal sum." John Folk was one happy church treasurer.

Bert breathed easily. John hadn't a clue regarding what Bert knew.

They sat in happy companionship, contemplating how to spend this munificent amount of cash; there were so many needs. Folk cleared his throat and said timidly, "Pastor, would it look greedy, or preemptive, if we put some of the money in our roof fund and deposited the rest in the church's general account?"

Bert looked at him, thought a moment, and nodded. "Yeah, why don't you do that, just in case..." He let the sentence trail off. Their concerns ran in the same direction. Above all else, the roof was priority number one.

"How much will it take to finish the roof, John?"

"Probably $10,000," Folk replied.

"Yeah go ahead...make that deposit in the roof fund. No one can object, the money's still in the church's name."

More silence. "Who's on Building Maintenance this year? Can't remember who rotated off and who came aboard."

"Let me check." John opened his cell. "I fuss over gadgets taking over our minds and here I am using one to get info I should know. Yeah, here we go. Jim Simons and Carl Atkins are the new guys on building maintenance."

"Know anything about them, John?"

"Not really, only that they're in that line of work; dealing with fixing things is their business."

"Could you call them? See if they could meet here tonight. I'd like to get something started before news of this windfall reaches ears that may have different spending priorities than ours."

John's face blanched knowingly. "I'll call as soon as I get to the office; set up a meeting for tonight around 7. That OK with you?"

"Yeah, fine, but better make it 7:30...that'll give them time to get home and eat before coming."

"Sure Pastor. Incidentally, what are your top priorities? I want to be on the same page when we start prioritizing church needs."

"No doubt about the roof, that's priority one. I'd say our parking lot's a disgrace with holes developing into craters. Bad on people's tires and on folks' feet."

"Amen," said John. "If I may suggest a third, the carpet in the sanctuary is not only an eyesore, but a hazard as well. I've seen women catch their heels in threadbare places and almost fall."

"Bring that up at the meeting John. It's a good suggestion."

Before leaving for the day, Bert asked Ruth to fix coffee and set the timer for 7 p.m.

"I can come back, Pastor, no problem."

"No, no, it won't be necessary; just put the timer on...it'll be okay. Thanks anyway," reassured Bert.

Jim Simons and Carl Atkins were not two peas in a pod. Simons, short, rotund, with muscles like steel, was part owner of a building maintenance company. Atkins was tall, lean, near spitting image of the old comedian Stan Laurel. Atkins was foreman in a construction company. He loped rather than walked into the office. Bert was pouring coffee when John arrived, carrying a plate of brownies.

"Shirley sent these to snack on," John explained. The men grinned and reached for one. The four sat quietly drinking coffee, praising Mrs. Folk's brownies. John beamed at their compliments.

Bert broke the repast. "John, you get started with the reason we're meeting."

John nodded, finished swallowing coffee, took the envelope from his inner pocket, and began reading its contents. Bert watched the two men's expressions as John reached the dollar amount involved. When John finished reading, Simons and Atkins in unison whistled. "Someone send this as a joke, John?"

Folks shook his head. "No, no, I've had it verified at our bank. It's legit, we can cash it anytime."

"Anyway we can find out who our angel is so we can thank him?" asked Atkins.

John shook his head. "No way; it's been tried by my bank manager; all details are blocked."

"Hey," said Simons philosophically, "if it's spendable, and the donor wants anonymity, we'll gladly comply. We'll do what he wants, fix up our sadly neglected building. Boy this is one for the books!"

Bert smiled. This was what he wanted, enthusiasm for repairing the building. He gave John the nod to continue.

"This brings us to the reason we're meeting," said John. "The donor gave Pastor full authority to prioritize building needs. However, Bert wants the committee to look over the church, asses its needs, and present your opinion as to what should be taken care of first, at a special church conference."

John Folk cleared his throat and said with some trepidation, "I'm asking before anything else is taken care of, that we fix the roof of the children's department. I've asked Bert if we could set aside money for that project before anything else. He has agreed."

"You got my vote on that," said Simons. "My kid complains about his Sunday School room every time it rains."

"Yeah, that's a priority that's gotta be addressed," Atkins chimed in. "And, we need to think seriously about fixing our parking lot," grumbled Carl. "I've messed up too many tires on those holes."

The others nodded in agreement.

"What would a new parking lot cost?" asked Bert.

"Let me get a figure on that," offered Jim Simons. Construction was his game. "I know guys in cement, might able to get us a deal."

Bert saw the opportunity and seized it. "Jim, would you be willing to get some figures, line up a good contractor, and oversee the job?"

Jim Simons paused and thought for a moment. "Yeah, Pastor, I could do that. It's what the building committee's supposed to do, right?" The men nodded.

Bert breathed a sigh of relief; the committee overseeing the projects, spending the money, and his hands staying away from directing any of this. Perfect.

The rest of the evening was spent assessing needs, comparing one need against another. But the idea of roof, parking lot, and carpet were fixed in their minds. Bert felt sorry for the committee. They had no idea the obstruction they would encounter from those who saw church NEEDS through colored glasses.

They closed the meeting in prayer, agreeing that the check was a miracle from God. A conference would be set for two weeks. By then Atkins and Simons would inspect, and get bids on the projects they planned to present to the congregation.

"One thing before you go," said Bert. "I caution you not to say anything about the check, not even to your wives. If it gets out that there's money in our account, our plans for the church's needs could be jeopardized." Bert looked at them to see if they caught the inference.

Simons and Adkins exchanged glances and nodded. "Oh yeah, preacher...we understand."

Jim and Carl left first. John and Bert took the empty cups into the kitchen. "Ready to leave, Bert?"

"Yeah, I'm ready, but I've something to fill your ears with." John looked startled. They began walking toward Bert's car. "Alice and I are getting married. Do you think you could chair the conference, or should I ask Bob Billingsly? Alice and I'll leave early next Monday morning for Raleigh. Dr. Hinton's going to marry us."

John grinned with genuine pleasure and grabbed Bert's hand, shaking it vigorously. "That's great news Bert, you need someone by your side; it's tough going it alone." His enthusiasm took Bert by surprise. Folk was not known for exuberance regardless of the situation. Bert was touched. He respected John, was grateful for his loyalty and dedication to taking care of church finances without charging a dime.

"I'll be taking a month's Sabbatical. I'll see to my replacement and get back to you. My house can accommodate them, if he brings his wife. Mrs. Jackson will see to their meals."

"This is God's timing, Bert. No problem about expenses now." Economics were always uppermost in this Scot's mind. They parted company, John in happy contemplation over the new roof, Bert happily anticipating his forthcoming wedding.

Alice called that evening, and Bert filled her in on the day's events. When he mentioned the check, she made no comment, and he was wise enough to keep his curiosity buttoned up. He mentioned the meeting with the building committee, the setting of repair priorities, and John Folk agreeing to chair the proposed conference.

"We'll be out of the state when the church meeting takes place. At least we'll be spared the agony of sitting through that. Simons and Atkins are strong men, they won't be pushed around. Of that I'm certain." Alice listened, then changed the subject to his Sabbatical plans. Bert obliged.

"I have everything under control and my replacement is Rev. Clarence Butler, retired minister from Georgia. He and his wife will live in the house. So, honey, what time do you get back from New York on Sunday?" She told him and he said he'd meet her plane. "Can't wait to hold you honey...miss you every minute of the day."

Sleep was easy that night. He'd killed a dozen birds with one little stone. The exercise had tired him out.

CHAPTER THIRTEEN

Mary/Martha Chapel was even lovelier than Alice had expected. She thought of the shoddy place where her first marriage had taken place, and shuddered. This tiny chapel had a capacity for fifty at people at most, in its serendipitous white and red interior. A maroon runner divided the chapel into two sections. Both pulpit and organ sat on a white platform. On the floor, left of the pulpit, was a baby grand piano. Everything was pristine, even to its gentle fragrance of honeysuckle.

Alice, in an off-white chiffon tea length gown with a beaded bodice, sparkled as she walked the aisle to meet Bert. Bert stood by the altar watching her every advancing step, smiling through moist eyes. Soft organ music kept rhythm to the swish of her lovely gown. Her heart was singing; she'd never been happier. Alice wore a little head veil barely covering her eyes, secured by a circle of pink rose buds. Her golden sandals trod softly, rhythmically, to the organ's rendition of Mendelssohn's bridal music. At the altar she slipped her arm through Bert's and handed her bouquet of red roses to her attendant. Dr. Hinton looked dignified in ministerial robes of white. The simple ceremony moved Alice to tears that cascaded down her cheeks.

Mrs. Hinton hosted the lovely wedding breakfast following the nuptials. The church family couldn't have been more gracious to the couple. Congratulations flowed like fragrant coffee as they ate the sumptuous brunch before taking off for Charleston where they spent their wedding night and remained there for a week before traveling to New York. They toured Charleston leisurely, seeing famous landmarks suggested in a brochure at the bed and breakfast they stayed at.

Alice was eager to show Bert places of interest in New York where she'd grown up, so before embarking in business, they took in a couple of good plays, dined at luxurious restaurants, and stayed at the Ritz Carlton.

The third week Alice put on her business hat and called David Carpenter to set up a meeting at his office for the following Monday at 3 p.m. She scheduled a meeting with Mr. Thornton for Monday before noon.

Bert was aware of the change in Alice as she took on the role of head of Darlington Enterprises. She was Alice with him; Allison to the Darlington conglomerate–the ultimate business woman. He was taken aback, but he was proud.

Al Thornton rose when Allison entered his office. His tongue hadn't finished greeting her, when a distinguished gentleman followed her in, and shut the door behind them. Thornton waved them to chairs and waited for an introduction.

"Mr. Thornton, I'd like you to meet my husband, Rev. Robert Davenport. I was his secretary the seven years I was hiding from George." Turning to Bert she said, "Honey, this is Mr. Albert Thornton, George's attorney, who has been extremely helpful to me since taking over Darlington Enterprises."

Bert rose and stretched his hand over Thornton's desk. The lawyer rose awkwardly, confused with the husband status, and grasped Bert's outstretched hand. His foot pressed the button signaling his secretary to bring in coffee and record the meeting.

They heard a discreet knock and Vera entered, carrying a tray with three cups of coffee, sugar and cream. Thornton introduced her to the new bridegroom. Bert smiled warmly and shook her hand. Vera returned the smile and left the room, impressed.

Bert sat quietly ingesting the conversation between Allison and Thornton. He knew nothing about stocks and bonds, but was acquainted with businesses in general. He sipped his coffee and listened, his eyes on his bride. Discussion of stocks, bonds, shares, edges, etc. grew wearisome. Bert tuned them out and turned to events of the past few weeks. He marveled that Alice had consented to marry him, especially after her inheritance.

The meeting took on a new tone that got Bert's attention. "Were you able to get the new will drawn up?" Allison asked.

Thornton nodded. "The will is made according to your instructions, waiting to insert the name of the beneficiary you said you'd provide when you came to the office."

"That's fine," said Allison. "You can fill in the name of Robert J. Davenport, my husband, as beneficiary of my estate. I will add a codicil regarding paintings, personal items, and so forth, plus a few trusts for Mona and her family later. I want to make certain that the bulk of my estate goes to my husband at my decease."

Alice did not look at Bert, who in turn did not know where to look. He was embarrassed and wondered if Thornton thought he'd put Alice up to this. He couldn't protest; it would be a useless gesture, and undercut Alice's ability to make decisions. He kept his cool and his tongue where it belonged, behind closed lips.

"The will is drawn. I'll have Vera type in the name." Using the intercom, Thornton summoned his secretary. In short order the name of Robert J. Davenport was applied to the new will and witnessed by Vera and the receptionist in the outer office. The will was handed to Allison in a leather pouch. She thanked the lawyer and put it into her capacious bag. Bert stood mute, glad she hadn't handed it to him. The reverend was embarrassed anew when he shook Thornton's hand, and was glad to get out of the attorney's office.

"I understand you have a meeting with David Carpenter this afternoon," Thornton said as he escorted them out of his office into the reception area.

Alice nodded. "Thanks for taking care of the will for me."

"My pleasure, Mrs. Davenport," said a thoughtful Al Thornton.

He stood looking after them, then returned to his office. Vera entered shortly carrying a tray with two coffees and a plate of sandwiches. "You look like you could use fresh caffeine and something to eat." He nodded gratefully. They were more than boss and secretary; an open secret everyone in the firm knew about.

"What'd you think of the husband?" he asked, biting into a sandwich.

Vera tapped her fingers on his desk, trying to gather her thoughts into an accurate assessment of Bert. "From the two glances I got of him, I'd say he is in love with her, not her money. Doesn't strike me as the kind that chases the green stuff."

"Yeah, my sentiments exactly. He just sat and listened. At times I felt his boredom. He was genuinely surprised, flushed a beet red, when the subject of the will came up. He was in love with her long before she became Mrs. Moneybags." He suddenly clapped his hands and began laughing.

"What's so funny?" asked Vera.

"Wait till David Carpenter meets the groom," Thornton chuckled. "He's going to get the disappointment of his life."

"How so?"

"Oh c'mon, Vera. You know our aging lothario's been angling to impress lady bountiful. One of our guys sees him working out at the gym most mornings. He's trying to tighten his flabby gut and get rid of one of his chins. When I think of David Carpenter running Darlington Enterprises, I'm grateful to the Reverend for stealing the prize. Allison may be brokerage smart, but she'd be easy picking for a smart con looking for an easy retirement berth. The pastor is no fool, didn't go to school just to eat his lunch. In his profession he's bound to have dealt with as many characters as any psychiatrist. He'll separate the chaff from the wheat, if anyone tries to scam his lady love. At first I resented his intrusion, but the more I think of it, we're all in safer hands with the Rev. Robert. J. Davenport next to the helm."

Vera, munching a sandwich, nodded contemplatively. "I think you're right. At least we won't have to wonder if he's stealing from the cookie jar." He looked at her and nodded.

At Allison's entrance, David Carpenter rose to greet her with a smile that stretched from ear to ear. It shrank slowly at the sight of a well-groomed man following in her wake.

"David," said Allison without preamble, "I'd like you to meet my husband, Rev. Robert Davenport." Turning to Bert, she said, "Honey, meet David Carpenter. He's George's business manager and has been very helpful in acquainting me with the business."

David had difficulty reaching Bert's outstretched hand. The limp handshake belied the strength that lay behind Carpenter's physique.

Carpenter barely heard a word Allison said; he was still in shock that another guy had stolen the husband designate that he'd been prepping for himself. He came out of his pique, and grinned toothily. "Sit down, sit down," he urged almost frantically. Seated behind his desk, David let his paunch hang loose; it sighed appreciatively.

"So," David began, trying to sound cool, cheerful. "How long have you known Mrs. Darlington?" he inquired. It would have been gauche to ask when Bert found out about her loot.

Bert knew a dig when he met one; considered the man, then felt sorry for him. Carpenter had aspired to the office of husband, and had been displaced by Bert.

"Seven years, when Alice fled New York and answered my help wanted ad for a church secretary. My wife was very sick; Alice took over the office. So, we've known each other for a long time. Right honey?" He smiled at Alice, reached and took her hand, brought it to his lips.

David Carpenter knew he'd made a serious faux pas. The pastor was a principled man, and he'd offended his sense of propriety. Fences had to be mended posthaste, or he just might find himself outside Darlington Enterprises, looking in.

"Sorry, Reverend, I was out of line; my curiosity just got way ahead of my manners. Please forgive my faux pas."

"Yes, of course," said Bert graciously. "You were interested in my wife's welfare."

David nodded, grateful for the second chance.

They finished discussing necessary business, and Allison and Bert left his office without fanfare. The moment they had gone, Carpenter was on his cell phone.

Tracking down Carl Stevens was easy; he was on the golf course feeling good about his game. David, still smarting from being replaced as groom, shot out curtly. "Bag your clubs and get in touch with your buddies. We need to meet and meet now in my office."

"Hey! What's your problem, Carpenter? What's going on?"

Carpenter ignored his question and stated between gritted teeth, "Your stalling tactics are over. Allison Darlington has a brand-new husband, a pastor at that. And for your information, he's no dummy. They just left my office. If you think you guys can wait her out, string her along with sales pending, think again. The balance of this discussion will not take place over the phone. Get Greene and Stokes, and be here as soon as possible."

Stevens found himself holding an empty cell. He wasn't alarmed, but he was concerned.

Chapter Fourteen

"Thank YOU, sir!" The waiter pocketed the large tip and carried Bert's breakfast tray from the posh suite, happily.

"You're welcome," said Bert Davenport, expansively.

Looking out the huge widows from their suite, Bert watched energy in motion in a city that never sleeps. He marveled at the skyscrapers and the unbelievable skyline of architectural beauty. People, like ants, moved in lines in and out of buildings, crossing streets, dodging traffic. Matchbox cars moved slowly in regimental fashion in the street below. Stop! Go! Cars jerked impatiently, heading for a multitude of destinations. Bert shook his head, and wondered how people endured such restriction of movement. He felt like the country mouse visiting the city, and in spite of the marvels it offered, he'd be glad to return to a dull existence in his quiet city. New York was definitely not his cup of tea, or coffee.

Bert glanced around the luxurious suite, taking pleasure in the comfort it gave him. He was no longer plagued with guilt that Alice's money was paying for these luxuries. When irritant thoughts surfaced, he bashed them down. God had provided this, why should he feel guilty enjoying it? But a tinge of unease nagged at his spirit, and when he turned from the window his spirit was grieved. Guilt sat heavily on him. As a counselor, he searched for a reason for his sudden altered mood, and rehearsed everything that had taken place that morning. He'd stayed put in the suite while Alice and Mona went shopping. There were no phone calls that morning to upset him. He'd had no visitors; talked to no one but the waiter.

Then he realized his unease. The opulent surroundings had suckered him into donning the robe of a guy so rich that he could give a tip to a waiter for picking up a tray, that could keep the Brown family in groceries for a week. Bert was disgusted with his hubristic behavior. He'd stepped out of character. And for what? For an exuberant thanks? He shook his head in disgust at selling his integrity for the price of a tip. "Keep back thy servant from presumptuous sin," he begged God.

A sudden need to connect with his church seized him; he dialed Mike. "Mike, it's Pastor. How are things going? How's Rev. Butler doing? How did the conference go?"

"Bert? Hey, pastor, I didn't expect to hear from you till you got home. You're still on honeymoon time. How's Alice, anyway?"

"Fine, fine! She's with her sister. They're tagging furniture and things she's sending to our Springer house. They'll go shopping later. I'd forgotten that women never tire of shopping." He laughed, delighted that he had a wife to tease about shopping.

"How's work on the church coming along? Is the roof fixed? What about the parking lot and the sanctuary? Can't wait till we get home."

Mike hesitated before answering. "Things are okay. The people have taken to Rev. Butler, but they miss you and keep asking when you and Alice are coming home. The parking lot's finished; Simons got us a good deal. John kept after the roofers till they hired extra men just to get him off their back. The church looks like it's got a new hairdo with the new roof. What a difference it makes. You'll be pleased with what's been done."

"Good, good to hear that. How's the carpeting coming along?" A pall of silence was all Bert got. "Hey Mike, you still there? Or has your battery died on you?"

"Nah, I'm here, Bert. Let's wait till you come home to catch up with the rest of the news. Sound good?"

"OK with me, but Alice is anxious to know if the color she picked for the carpet was acceptable."

"Oh yeah, tell her the color's great." Silence.

Bert hadn't been pastor for years without learning to read messages written in silence.

"You're holding out on me, little buddy. We don't do that to one another. My sixth sense just kicked in; what's going on that you're being coy about?"

"Awe, Bert I'd rather wait till we are in the same room."

"Give it to me straight, Mike. I'm a big boy; what's going on?"

Mike sighed. "Well, since you insist. Our bank account's frozen; John and Bob can't write checks."

"WHAT?! That's ridiculous! Our credit's good, and we've got plenty of money in the bank!" Bert stopped abruptly. "Sorry Mike, I shouldn't interrupt your explanation. So what's up? Tell me nice and easy, and don't hold anything back."

Mike cleared his throat. Bert waited impatiently. "Two deacons went to the bank with signature cards accompanied by a letter purporting to be from the trustees, stating that these men were the newly elected finance committee members and their signatures replaced the existing ones, and that John's and Billingsley's were obsolete. Right now, neither John nor Bob can sign any checks. It was a slick operation. We wouldn't have found out about it if the foreman working on the sanctuary hadn't asked John for a draw. When the foreman presented the check, the bank refused it…wrong signatures. John went tearing to the bank. He knows the bank president and demanded to know what was going on. It was then they discovered the switch. A bank clerk had taken care of the transaction; everything seemed in order. As the bank president told John, they are bankers, not interrogators. Churches change signature cards all the time. John is spitting nails. He wants that carpet down before that gang spends the balance in the bank for their idea of updating the sanctuary."

"Anything done in the auditorium?"

"Yeah, the pews are out; they're sitting in the hallways outside the sanctuary and in rooms that can hold some. It's a mess. John insists that the company finish the work, and promised them the money'll be there when they're finished laying the carpet."

"Has the carpet been purchased, Mike?"

"Well, it just so happens the foreman knew of a company liquidating its stock. The color we wanted was available at a great price. He bought it right off. Saved us a few thousand bucks. And we don't have to write a check for it, we can give him cash when we get it. It's stored at his warehouse. We lucked out there, Bert."

"How's John handling the offerings? I know he's not putting 'em in the bank."

"Oh no! The trustees count the money, and put it in canvas bank pouches. It's verified, dated, and John puts it in that old wall safe in his office. He's alerted the police chief and the police are keeping an eye on the church in their nightly drive-by surveillance. The police have been more than accommodating."

There was a noise at the door. Bert said hastily, "Alice's home. Call John, tell him you filled me in, and that I'll be home asap." He hung up his cell.

Bert headed to the door and took the packages from Alice, put them in a chair, and took her in his arms, kissing her warmly. "Missed you honey. Get your stuff tagged at the house?"

Alice nodded wearily, and snuggled closer to him. "Any coffee left? Or shall I call room service?"

Bert brought her what was left of the coffee he'd made. Alice sat beside him on the sofa, shoes off, wiggling her toes, sipping coffee and sighing. "I'm glad that ordeal's over. I don't want to go back to that house again... too many memories of George. The papers are signed, and the things I tagged will be shipped to South Carolina in a few days." They sat on the sofa lost in private thoughts. Alice handed him her empty cup. "Thanks, honey. How was your morning?"

"OK, I guess," he said without enthusiasm.

She rested her head on his shoulder and looked up into his face. "Something's bothering you Bert...you're not your jovial self. What is it?"

"Alice, we're still on our honeymoon, remember! Plenty of time ahead to deal with other things." He pointed at the packages for distraction. "So, what did you buy honey? My curiosity's piqued." His teasing regarding her shopping fell flat; his jovial bantering was missing.

Alice sat up straight and said determinately, "Bert we're not starting our marriage hiding things from each other, so give!"

He sighed, shook his head, and reached for her. Alice refused to be distracted. "Level with me, before I feel left out of whatever's going on that's bothering you."

"Alice, honey, I'm not leaving you out, I just don't want to spoil our honeymoon."

"If it bothers you, then of course it's time to discuss whatever it is."

With his arms around her, Bert told her what Mike had said about the frozen church funds. Alice was breathing hard when he finished. Silence encapsulated moments, then Alice was on her feet. Bert looked up, startled.

"Find out when the next plane leaves for home," she said curtly. "I'm going to pack; you do the same after you phone the airlines." She headed to the other room to gather her belongings.

"Alice, Alice!" He followed her into the bedroom. "We can't cut our honeymoon short; this problem isn't going anywhere. We'll deal with it when we get home. Let's not be hasty and...."

"Bert, I'm packing. Those cretins had a head start with you out of town. Now, call the airline, don't spend time arguing."

Bert grinned happily as he watched the helpmeet God had given him go into action. He called the airport.

The CEOs sat scowling at David Carpenter, seated upright behind his huge mahogany desk. Equal in rank, David had the edge; he was Darlington Enterprises' money man, the deal maker, the benefactor of the oligarchy. Stevens was irritated at being called from his golf game.

"You sounded like Chicken Little. The sky is falling! What's going on?" he asked waspishly. Greene and Stokes sat waiting. This was not Carpenter's normal behavior. "Bet it's the boss lady that's got your pants in a twist," continued Stevens impatiently.

Carpenter shrugged dismissively, splayed his hands in mock helplessness, leaned forward, elbows on desk, and said, "Yep, you guessed it Carl, it's the boss lady. You have two weeks from today to come up with a sale or a potential one, to dispose of your overseas companies. The woman's serious about divesting Darlington from European markets. If you refuse, or drag your feet hoping she'll change her mind, Allison says she will personally contact each country's U.S. ambassador and make a deal to sell our investment to them for one dollar. Which means you'll be out of a fat commission."

Deafening silence followed as Carpenter's words ran riotously through their stricken minds. Stevens rose to his feet and paced the floor. "Is she crazy? Doesn't she know how much our overseas investments bring into the company's coffers?" He paced some more, sat down, and glared at Carpenter.

"I'm just the messenger, Carl, I didn't write the script," David said dryly. "The new boss is convinced Europe will implode, more so now with all the refugees flooding their borders; draining resources, bankrupting them. She believes the European nations will nationalize; absorb foreign investments. Outsiders like us will lose our companies without compensation. We get out before the stampede begins, is her theory."

"That's crazy," said Stevens. "What's she drinking, or what kind of crazy website is she visiting? Our investments are well protected against nationalization." Stevens looked at his peers, hoping for backup, but found them in mute mode. "So," he jeered, "you're buying this crap from a lady whose knowledge of marketing is zero to zilch? Or don't you care about the fat bonuses you get every quarter? Let's see if she goes through with her threat to sell direct to the countries involved." He strode to the door, looked back at his colleagues, and aimed his parting shot at David.

"I thought you were going to work your alpha male charm on her, save our bacon. What happened? Did she not find you attractive?"

"Don't add crudity to immaturity, Carl. The lady has acquired a husband since I last saw her. A reverend no less, who comes across as alpha minister, one who doesn't sway with the wind."

Stevens flushed scarlet, and left, his last comment a slammed door.

The remaining men sat chewing decisions internally. Greene finally stood and sauntered to the huge window overlooking Manhattan. Without turning his head he said quietly, "Whether Mrs. D is right or wrong, I'm going to see what kind of a deal I can make. I'm tired of the hustle to do business across the globe; tired of exchanging my life for making the company more dough so that my retirement will be fatter. Hell, I may not live to see a retirement with all that's going on in the world. Could be her husband's influencing her. Whatever. I'm getting out; maybe this is what I needed, to really get out...start being a family man again. This is going to make Miriam's day. Go back to church with her, do a little singing of hymns I still find comforting. Life's too short to waste it gathering; gathering things you're gonna leave behind for someone else to squabble over. So tell the lady I'll get back to her shortly with some kind of a deal." He jingled keys and change in his pocket, and suddenly seemed at ease.

Carpenter looked at the tall figure with a slight stoop, hair completely gray, still in his early 50s. This was the first time Greene had ever unburdened himself. David was moved, and admired the guy's honesty.

Stokes was rotund, genial; smiling came easy to him. His demeanor now was somber. He'd listened intently to Greene. As if the ball had been passed to him, he spoke wearily. "I'm with Greene. I'm not clairvoyant, but you'd have to be deaf and blind not to notice that something's rotten in Europe. It's going crazy...and it's not without precedent. Nations have nationalized under duress. I've a pigeon in mind who just might jump at the offer I'll be making. So tell lady boss she'll be hearing from me soon."

Carpenter didn't take time to analyze what had taken place. When Greene and Stokes left, he reached for his landline. "Allison, Carpenter here...."

Mike was waiting for them at the airport and drove them to Alice's apartment. After seeing her settled, Mike drove Bert to Springer Avenue to pick up his car. Before leaving New York, Bert had phoned Rev. Butler, informing him of their change in plans; they'd be coming home that day.

"Good to hear that, brother," said Clarence. "Something's come up at home that needs my attention. This works out fine. It's been great for us, but you're needed here."

Mike and Bert noticed suitcases and boxes sitting on the front porch as the car approached the house. Bert exited Mike's vehicle as Clarence put a box in the trunk, then wiped his hands on his trouser legs and walked to Bert, hand outstretched. "Hail to the new bridegroom," Clarence grinned, shaking Bert's hand warmly.

"Thanks," said Bert, blushing a little. "I couldn't have asked for a greater bride." The men finished emptying the porch luggage into the car and went into the house. Their noses led them to the kitchen where Connie Butler was pouring three mugs of coffee, having witnessed Bert's arrival.

"Congratulations Bro. Davenport. Where's the bride? I've yet to meet her."

"Unpacking at the apartment, but you'll meet her at the next conference. I don't intend to let her out of my sight now that I've found

119

her." He grinned, sipping coffee. They sat at the kitchen table talking, avoiding the subject uppermost in their minds: the church schism facing Bert.

"Clarence, you've been around my people for a month. Do you have a sense of how folks are leaning with the issue of change? Don't hesitate to be frank; I need clarification as to what's been going on in my absence. What's your assessment of the mood of my flock?"

Butler was loath to give Bert an answer. He prayed silently for wisdom. Nothing but the truth would help; no placebo would change the fissure in Fair Haven. Butler knew the vagaries of church folk. Although their souls were right with God, the carnal nature was always ready to be contrary with issues not worth bothering about. Satan has a proclivity for directing people's minds from important matters, to mindless trivia. Anything to keep turmoil in the church. Butler was thankful his days of shepherding were over. He doubted he could go through what Bert was facing. To the Rev. Butler, modernized churches lacked the ambience of worship; loud, discordant music irritated his soul. Thank God he'd finished his course. Church splits not only robbed ministers of restful nights, but of time better spent in doing the work of the ministry—getting souls ready to meet their Maker.

Bert watched Clarence sip his coffee, and asked, "Clarence, do you think there's room for compromise?"

Butler sighed and answered, "I'll be blunt Bert, you've got a clique that's determined to get rid of you, because they're convinced you're the one keeping the church from growing. You're their albatross. I was there one week when I knew who your enemies were. Your congregation's mostly behind you, but they're getting tired of worshiping in a hostile atmosphere. People come to find peace, not more of the same thing they deal with daily. But, the agitators are accusing you of pulling a fast one with that donor's check. Resent it that you were too quick for them to get in their two cents concerning the spending of the money. They would have used it to bring the church up to what they believe a 21st century church should look like. Everyone agreed they needed the new roof and the parking lot. Not much said about the carpet, but the dissenters keep stoking the furnace, saying the people should have been consulted before any money was spent on any project, and ignoring the advice of the building committee."

The Rev. Butler looked at Bert. "I didn't ask where the money came from; none of my business. But I am curious."

Bert smiled weakly. "Clarence, the money came through the mail as a gift from an anonymous donor. The letter that accompanied a check for $50 thousand gave me full authority to spend the money on the needs of the church, as I saw fit. But rather than go ahead and get things done without consulting anyone, I, my treasurer, and two men on the building and maintenance committee met and prioritized the church's needs. The roof on the children's building leaked, so that was an absolute necessity. Our parking lot was a mess, another priority, and the sanctuary carpet is long overdue for replacement. At the church meeting, the treasurer read the donor's letter informing the people that authority for spending the money was given to the pastor. Building and Maintenance announced their findings: roof, parking lot, and carpet should be dealt with first. The vote to go along with the recommendations of the committee were accepted overwhelmingly.

"So, Bro. Butler, the gift that was hailed as a blessing, now seems to have turned into a curse." He looked ruefully at his colleague.

Connie, seated across from the men, shook her head. "You got the roof fixed, the parking lot fixed, and you'll get the carpet down somehow. I'll wager that that $50,000 would be buying computer and sound equipment, new lighting, and jazzing up the sanctuary, if you hadn't been one step ahead of the progressives."

She picked up the empty cups and looked at her watch. "We'd better get started Clarence. I'd like to be home before dark."

Butler nodded and rose from the table. He needed to talk to Bert. He reached for his jacket from the back of the kitchen chair and put it on. Bert followed them to their car. Connie was getting into the passenger's seat when her cell rang. Clarence closed her car door and stepped toward Bert. "You were within your right to use that gift the way the donor indicated. But however innocent your action, it was misconstrued by troublemakers. They allege the people were denied their right to vote on other suggestions as well. Connie's right, they would be spending the money their way, leaky roof be damned. They're determined to get their hands on what's left of the money. They'll stop at nothing."

Bert grimaced. "Yeah, I got ahead of God; I used the leverage the donor gave me, instead of letting the Spirit do His work at the conference. Truth is, I was afraid the opposition would get their mitts on the money, so I maneuvered it my way. Perhaps I've created a mess worse than it needed to be."

Clarence glanced in his car; Connie was still talking animatedly on her cell. "Brother Davenport, you asked if compromise would work. It depends on what you mean by compromise, what you're willing to bring to the table, and what you expect the other side to give up."

Bert had given little thought to the extent of compromise he'd be willing to accept, and what he would reject. "I've only begun thinking about it Clarence. I've no idea what that would even look like."

Clarence nodded. "Bert, what if both sides have compromised? The church hasn't split, but it hasn't grown either. Supposing a committee comes to you and tells you your sermons on sin, repentance, and so forth are old school, that you should lighten up, preach more social gospel, and the millennials will start coming. The committee suggests your sermons be more reflective of issues people are dealing with, and encourages you to leave off the heavy stuff about salvation. What will you do then? The new age churches look alike, but not all are as progressive as others. Some do preach the gospel, along with the 21st century trappings. But compromise is an unknown quality, and you've no idea where it'll lead you. Let's face it Bert; the traditional church is struggling to maintain its doctrine in a culture that brands everything that's traditional as obsolete and should be pitched and let fresh ideas in."

Bert stared at him, shook his head wearily, and remarked, "Yeah, Clarence, I see your point. Compromise would be like blackmail; it would be I who prevented growth regardless of what the church gave up. Progressives never look inward; it's always the other guy's fault, whatever the cause. So, that kind of compromise isn't an option. Keep me in your prayers Clarence. I need them."

Butler nodded, and walked closer to his car. Connie was winding down and waving him to get into the car. Clarence chuckled. "Can't believe that a woman who weighs a little over 100 lbs dictates my every move." He laughed, and Bert joined him in the observation of wives' power over their husbands.

He watched as the Butlers merged with road traffic; watched till they were out of sight.

That afternoon, Ed Brown and several other helpers took away the old bedroom set. In its place stood the beautiful bedroom furniture Alice had purchased in New York. They were settling in. She wisely decided to change and add to the present house rather than raise eyebrows by moving into a new home. Furniture, paintings, object d'art from her home in the big city eventually turned Bert's house into an impressive place.

Bert was on the phone with Alice when Mike arrived. Bert held up the empty coffee pot, and mouthed "COFFEE." Mike nodded and complied while Bert finished his conversation with Alice. Mike put coffee mugs on the kitchen table.

Bert said wearily, "Mike, my life's revolving around coffee pots and pastries. Good thing it's not around the bottle." They laughed in agreement.

"Well, let's have the whole story; I've heard it piecemeal from Brother Butler; it's time I heard the whole nine yards from you."

Mike shrugged and bit into a Danish. "Well, you know they forged signature cards for the bank and cut John and Bob out of check signing for the church." Bert nodded.

"I never knew John Folk to have such a temper. He marched into the bank president's office and wasn't about to leave until he found out what happened. Of course the bank had nothing to do with it and the banker told John it was church business; not the bank's. John later apologized to the bank president; they're old friends, you know."

Bert grinned, thinking of mild-mannered John. "Yeah, he's coming over tonight along with Atkins and Simons. Plan on being here." Mike nodded. "The guy that's laying the carpet is joining us. My goodness, I thought I'd experienced every kind of shenanigan in church splits, but this beats all. A new kind of coup to get rid of the pastor." Bert took a sip of coffee.

Mike grinned. "I'm sure glad you're back. You have a knack for outwitting jerks. Must be ecclesiastical savvy that's built into your psyche. We've been trying to outwit them, but they seem to have more wits that we do, 'cause they outwit us."

Bert shrugged dismissively. "We'll see if sneaky gets the job done. So who exactly is involved?"

Mike drew out a small notebook, flipped pages, and read some names.

"What about the Board of Trustees, any of them defect to the miscreants?"

Mike consulted his notes. "Yeah, two who were elected at last Conference. Stan Williams and Jason Barnes."

Bert nodded. "It figures; those two are the youngest. Where are our members in general in the midst of this?"

"Some are ready to leave the ship...fed up. Can't say I blame them. Who wants to come to church for worship and have to endure this childish behavior? They want to run good people off and blame you for emptying the church because of your refusal to compromise."

"Take last Wednesday night, for instance. Prayer meeting was going when those dissenters met in the parking lot. We could see their car lights through that portion of glass block. They met and came in together as one body; sat in the back middle section. Then the noise began: shuffling feet, coughing, clearing throats, whispering, laughing. A cacophony of disruptive sounds while Bro. Butler was preaching. But he just stopped, took a glass of water, and said icily and pointedly, 'If any of you need water or the nursery, I'll wait till your needs are met before turning our attention back to God's word.' So to answer your question, can you blame our people for being fed up, ready to leave?"

Bert was furious. "No, and by the grace of God, it's going to stop, if I have to fisticuff them in the parking lot."

Mike sighed and shook his head morosely. "Bert, they were rude several times to Rev. Butler. He always had a rejoinder, but I could tell some of their nasty got to him. How can those who say they're Christians act like that, especially in the house of God?"

"Mike, it's no mystery. Satan will use anyone who's willing to do his bidding. Even with the Holy Spirit in us, we often choose to ignore His leadership, and follow another that appeals to our carnal nature. We make choices till the day we die as to which spirit we're going to listen to. Christians cannot lose their salvation, but they certainly can lose peace here, and rewards in the hereafter.

"We need to get our people into the Word, Mike. The word of God in our hearts is our best defense; gives us the edge every time. 'Thy Word have I hid in mine heart that I might not sin against Thee!' We'll announce a special prayer meeting, Mike. We need God's help. I can't fight those malefactors alone. When Nehemiah and the exiles were rebuilding Jerusalem's wall, his biggest agitators were leaders in the Jewish community. History's replete with Christians being destroyed by their friends. Job's an example. His comfortless friends nearly destroyed him with wisdom."

Alice came into the kitchen; Mike rose to hug her. After a few exchanges, Mike left for home. "See you tonight, Pastor."

Alice's eyebrows rose. "You having a meeting here tonight, honey?"

"Yeah, things I've got to sort out with the men before Sunday service. Just a few guys: John, Mike, the guys from the building committee, and maybe Bob Billingsly."

Alice looked concerned. "Bert, you know money's no problem. If money lessens your burden, for goodness sake use it. It's God's money, for His church."

He put his arms around her and nuzzled her hair, smelling the fragrance of lilac shampoo. He heard her, but also knew money alone couldn't solve this problem. "I know darling, and it's a great comfort to know money's available. But I don't want to replace guidance from the Spirit with dependence on money. Money is ephemeral, but the Spirit's guidance is eternal." He kissed her soundly. "How I ever got you to marry me is a miracle," he murmured.

Alice stirred in his arms then withdrew. "I'd better see what's in the house for your men to snack on." She left to checked the pantry.

CHAPTER FIFTEEN

John Folk arrived first. Bert was shocked to see facial lines that hadn't been there when they'd last met. He took Bert's outstretched hand and shook it vigorously. "So good to see you, Pastor. This bank mess has been a nightmare from hell. They're killing the church Bert. Many of our good people are staying away. I'm glad you're back. How's Alice? Poor woman starting married life in the middle of a church mess."

"John, let's not panic. This is God's house, and the promise still stands that 'the gates of hell shall not prevail against it.'"

John Folk nodded, but doubt was in the nod. Already the miracle of the $50,000 check, forgotten. He wanted to hear Bert announce a plan that would cut the legs from under the conspirators. He gave short shrift to Bert's talk about leaning on the Spirit. He wanted a hands-on operation; impatient with the notion of a spiritual one. He sighed and said resignedly, "Yeah, Bert, but my faith's not what it should be, especially after tangling with Christians arguing their inane point of view in religious terms."

The doorbell rang. Alice's voice was heard welcoming arrivals. Mike and Jim Simons joined them in the family room. Carl Atkins and Joe Sullivan came next. Bob Billingsly brought up the rear.

The meeting began with Mike praying. "God, we're here because we need help from You. Just guide our minds, help us formulate ways to deal with those attempting to destroy our church. We're discouraged and need Divine intervention. Thank You for hearing us. In Jesus' name we pray, Amen."

Male voices repeated, "Amen."

Alice brought coffee and sandwiches to the family room. The pale green walls complimented the cream leather lounge chairs and couches. The opulent table lamps centered on mahogany end tables glowed softly on the gathering. An ambience of peace embraced the men as they relaxed over the snacks; it was a respite from the task of how to deal with the discord among the brethren. Peace was felt; anxiety subdued, and courage rose in the breasts of the men faced with the herculean task of bringing a congregation back together.

"Great coffee pastor," said Carl. The others joined in praise of Alice's coffee and sandwiches.

Bert smiled happily. "I'm one lucky guy; got the best wife on the planet. Not discounting your wives," he finished lamely. They laughed at his awkward comments.

In discussing the coup, John confessed, "It caught us off guard; never dreamed anyone was capable of such subterfuge."

"I'd put the scheme squarely in Hunt's lap," said Billingsly. "He's shrewd. Freezing our assets would be the top of the list in a banker's mind."

"Well, the milk's spilled," said Bert, "and we need to figure some way to mop it up. We're going ahead with our plans to get the carpeting laid in spite of this roadblock. Our congregation's going to walk on new carpet this coming Sunday morning. So let's see what we need to do to be able to meet that goal."

Bert turned to Joe. "Can you begin laying the carpet in the morning?"

"Sure, if I'm guaranteed cash to pay my crew when we're through."

"You have my word on that—it'll be there when the job's finished," Bert assured him.

"But our money's tied up Bert," protested John.

"I've arranged for a loan from someone who knows the score, knows we've got the money but it's tied up illegally. My party's willing to trust us." If they only knew, thought Bert.

"Luckily the carpet's in our warehouse," said Sullivan. "We've done our measuring, and the pews are out," he said, jotting down figures. "If we start cutting and laying carpet in the morning, we would have to spend all day Saturday putting the pews back in place...no small feat. I'd have to hire more carpenters to replace the pews to meet your deadline." He looked at Bert without apology, waiting for a reply.

"Go ahead, Joe, hire as many as you need," answered Bert firmly.

John Folk's eyes glazed over; he was about to equivocate, when Bert raised his hand. "Trust me John, the money'll be there when the work's finished."

John wiped his brow and laughed. "Am I about to see another miracle, Pastor?"

"Now for strategy," said Bert, changing hats. "Joe, can you move the carpet into the church tonight, unobserved?"

"Sure, if I have a key to get in, no problem."

Bert nodded. "We'll see to that. And, have your men park near the church but not in the parking lot so they won't draw attention to the fact that something's going on inside."

Sullivan grinned, enjoying a bit of intrigue. "Yeah, preacher. It'll add a little spice to the mundane job." The rest of the men chuckled in agreement.

With business over, the men relaxed in filial companionship unique with believers. Their leader was back, their goal was set, and God had provided a way for the sanctuary carpet to be laid. Bob Billingsly grinned and said, "I can visualize Greg Hunt's face when his feet tread that new sanctuary carpet Sunday morning. He'll have a conniption fit wondering where the money came from."

They were reluctant to leave but finally did, after thanking Alice for the refreshments. They could hardly wait for Sunday morning to come. Each conjured up in his mind what the dissidents would do when they walked on the maroon sea under their feet.

Domesticity had finally found its roots in the house on Springer Avenue. They sat together on the sofa after the men had taken their leave. Bert said elliptically, "You know honey, a scripture invaded my mind when they were discussing the split. Something Jesus said to His disciples. It's as true today as it was then."

Alice lifted her head from his shoulder. "Oh, and what popped into your head, Bert?"

He grinned down at her. "Jesus said, 'The poor ye have with you always.'"

Alice looked quizzical. "Meaning...?"

Bert ruffled her hair and said soberly, "I see parallelism here. 'Splits ye have with you always!'" He laughed. Alice shook her head; he tightened his hold on her.

It was Saturday, 7 p.m., when Sullivan called. "Preacher, it's ready for inspection. We've a gang here putting the pews back, and that's no small job considering putting them down on new carpet. I'll need the check for my guys. You want to come here or do I come to your place for the money?"

"Great! Great! We'll be right over." He put the phone in its cradle and called out, "Alice, Alice, the carpet's laid. They're putting the pews in place. I said we'd be right over."

Alice came into the hallway. He grabbed her and swung her around. "Let me tidy up," she said excitedly. "Won't take a minute."

Neither had visited the church since their return from New York. "We should stay away," Alice had advised. They had. Driving onto the new parking lot, and looking at the new roof, brought tears to Bert's eyes. He found himself thinking of Jenny's concern for the parking lot...she'd be so pleased. Turning to Alice, he asked, "What do you think, darling?"

She smiled and nodded. "It's like the church has a new hairdo and the parking lot a new beginning." Bert agreed. What transformation!

Sullivan met them in the sanctuary, expansive with praise for his men. "Preacher they worked harder on this job than on any job we've ever done before. What do you think?"

Bert and Alice looked at the beautiful maroon carpet, the platform, the blending of pews with the carpet. Alice had tears in her eyes. "It's perfect," she said quietly. "Just beautiful."

Sullivan nodded; he was touched. He knew the history behind the carpet, and admired the minister for overcoming obstacles and getting the job done. Bert handed Joe a cashier's check. "We added a bonus. You worked a miracle, Joe. Miracles are worth honoring."

Joe grinned appreciatively. "Oh ye of little faith," he said. "I confess I worried that you might not be able to get the cash." He shook Bert's hand vigorously, and went to find his men and give them checks he'd written ahead of time.

Before the men left, Bert and Alice thanked them personally. "We'll have service in the sanctuary this Sunday thanks to your hard work. If you don't have a church home, we would love to have you worship with us."

They nodded politely, and thanked Bert for his invitation.

As they left the room, he put his arms around Alice. "Your anonymous check led to this, honey."

"You guessed," she smiled teasingly.

"Come on now, who else would send us $50,000? Of course I knew. It was John's excitement over it that sent my pride to the garbage dump where it belonged. If God gave you that money, and I know He did, why not use it for His work? Look at our parking lot, look at this sanctuary. Honey, this is a miracle that only the Creator could produce."

He was kissing her when a voice shouted, "Hey now, none of that making out in God's house!" Mike was standing at the back, surveying the wonder of it all. "Boy oh boy, what a difference, what a difference!" He walked to the platform and looked over the pews. "Can't wait to see the happy faces sitting in those pews in the morning—at least most of them!" Going to the piano he fingered a chorus and in his baritone voice sang, "Isn't the love of Jesus something wonderful...wonderful, wonderful. Oh, isn't the love of Jesus something wonderful, wonderful it is to me." Jumping down from the platform he grabbed Bert's hand and pumped it vigorously. "Boy am I glad you're gonna be behind that pulpit in the morning. Well, gotta go; the gang's in the car. Heading for McDonald's. Ruth saw your car in the parking lot...that's why we stopped. See you in the morning." Mike was at the auditorium entrance when he turned and quipped, "You have my permission to resume your making out, padre."

Bert and Alice giggled as they made their way to pastor's office. A serious look came over Alice's face.

"Bert, remember how I said I had something in mind that I needed to think more about?"

"That seems like ages ago now, but yes, I remember," replied Bert curiously.

"Well, God is clearly behind this financial windfall for me—and now for us as a couple. I want to be able to use this money in a way that will honor him, but without changing how people treat us. If people knew how rich we are, they would never look at us the same way again. They'd either put us on a pedestal, or be running to us nonstop for financial help."

"Yes, I see your point," remarked Bert, brow furrowed.

"So," Alice continued, her face lighting up, "I want us to establish a secret foundation that can provide money to pastors like you, those who want to stay true to the Gospel but who are struggling to pay the bills. We can set up an application process to make sure that it's not just lip service, and that the money will be spent on specific, tangible ways to reach others for Christ. What do you think?"

"Alice, that is brilliant! That way we can help other churches like ours, but without letting on that Darlington Enterprises is the source of the funding. My mind is spinning just thinking about how many pastors would be so relieved to have help funding those great ideas that get left undone because the electric bill must come first. Sweetheart, I just don't deserve you. You are a rare gem."

Alice beamed with the recognition of her idea. "I can get things in motion very quickly; I'll have David Carpenter get everything in place and make sure that the financial source of the foundation is completely obscured. What do you think we should call it?"

Bert didn't have to think long. "What about Old Time Religion Foundation?"

Alice smiled. "I think that's perfect. OTR Foundation for short...that has a nice ring to it!" They headed home that night anxious about how things would play out the next day, but excited for how God might use the money in the bank for His glory.

Alice slipped into the second row of pews to the left of the podium with Ruth Anderson. People coming in from outside and from Sunday school gave her cover. Excited gushes could be heard from every person stepping into the sanctuary. "Well this was long overdue," commented one woman loudly. "Yeah, it's beautiful; makes you feel like you're in God's house," came the response. Human voices sounded like bees swarming around bee hives, waiting to release their spirited opinions.

Preacher was back; what did he have to say about everything that had happened in his absence? Some had gotten e-mails saying Bert was resigning this morning. "Where is he?" asked a concerned voice. "Pastor usually stands at the door greeting us."

Alice wondered how Bert was coping; he'd been nervous when she left him in his office. He hadn't slept well last night. She had said as they parted, "Please, Bert...just be yourself, everything will work out. I'll be praying for you, and I know John and Mike will be too."

"Well, three among a few hundred are good odds, honey," he replied as he'd kissed her before going to his desk.

Bert stayed there until he heard Sylvia at the piano. He breathed a prayer, straightened his tie, and walked to the pulpit as if to the gallows. He stopped at the auditorium door and surveyed the congregation as they stood singing "At Calvary." Bert walked down the right aisle to the platform. Heads turned as the congregants tried to reconcile the elegant figure passing them as the pastor they'd seen a month ago. Dressed in a tailored suit, Bert Davenport looked more like a wealthy financier than a country preacher. The subtle cologne that followed in his wake didn't go unnoticed. He nodded right and left but didn't stop to chat. Those close enough to see his feet as he mounted the platform observed his handmade leather shoes. His silk tie hadn't been bought in Safe Haven, that was for sure. It complimented his dark gray jacket and light gray slacks. Alice smiled to herself; he was her man. Dressed in expensive clothes added a new dimension, a new mystique to his persona.

The congregation had lost its place when it stopped to gawp at Bert, and had a time catching up with Mike. Bert glanced over at Mike, nodded, and sat down on his platform chair. Little did the congregation know that his legs were about to collapse under him from anxiety.

Mike next led the assembly in "There Is a Fountain." The congregation sang louder, their way of letting the preacher know they were glad he was back. From his peripheral view, Bert knew where men of interest were seated. He saw Ed Brown wipe his eyes with a handkerchief, and blow his nose. Bert loved the man who was considered a nobody by others; it was men like Ed that kept discouraged ministers from walking out. This diversionary thinking helped him get a grip on himself. He prayed silently, seeking help from the Holy Spirit for his sermon.

Mike was praying, heads were bowed. The ushers were passing the collection plates; Sylvia was playing softly. She's a good woman, thought Bert, consciously noting little things that he often missed.

Mike turned to Bert, nodded, and took his seat in the front pew to Bert's left. Bert rose and acknowledged Mike. "Thanks, Mike. Sylvia... beautiful music," He turned his attention to his parishioners. "Good to be back, good to see your smiling faces. God has showered blessings on this church. Just look at the carpet under your feet. Is it not beautiful?" The congregation broke out in amens and applauded till he held up his hand. "Alice and I saw the roof when we drove in. Looks like our church got a new hairdo." Laughter. "Kids won't be getting wet when it rains. Right?"

"Right, right," shouted Ed Brown.

"And how about that parking lot! Anyone sorry we have a new parking lot?"

There was silence for a moment until one man piped up, "Don't have to worry about blowing out a tire anymore, preacher!" That set the congregation applauding and nodding.

Bert had set the tone; the people acknowledged the blessings they'd received. "God sent us that money, and the donor wrote, 'Preacher, use it on the projects you feel are most beneficial to the people.' And we did!"

Bert knew when to stop beating a dead horse. "Now, turn in your Bibles to Ephesians 4:2. It's about time we mixed a little love into this sanctuary. Nothing can replace love. And believe you me, I'm a strong proponent of the stuff, especially since I made Alice my wonderful wife." Applause, and a smattering of laughter. Alice, looking beautiful in a black sheer wool suit, crimson silk blouse, and ruby earrings, blushed. Ruth leaned over and patted her hand and smiled, sensing her embarrassment.

Bert's voice was strong, his body felt no fatigue. He looked at Alice sitting beside Ruth and winked at her, then looked directly at his congregation.

Greg Hunt, sitting with Madeline and their ten-year-old son, had difficulty keeping bile from rising in his mouth. Walking on new carpet completely flummoxed him. When had it been laid? No one had mentioned any activity going on in the church. He paid no attention to Bert's sermon; he was too engrossed with unanswered questions. Who had paid for the carpet? How did the pews get back into position? Where did Bert come up with money for an outfit that cost big bucks? An evil spirit suggested maybe the check had been larger than $50 thousand. Yeah, that had to be it. Money didn't grow on trees. He grew impatient for the service to end so he could get with his gang and thrash out the money angle, especially Bert's new duds. Greg knew those rags cost a bundle.

Bert was speaking with new verve. Greg found it impossible not to listen.

"Tonight," commented the preacher, "I'll lay out plans for the church that I feel the Spirit is giving us. If you're here you'll get the full story; if not, you'll get someone else's version. After much prayer, I believe that God is moving the church in a new direction."

Bert closed the sermon with a plea for unity among the brethren. "A house divided cannot stand. We are the body of Christ; let us not tear our body limb from limb with our tongues." Bert turned to Mike, who led the congregation in that wonderful hymn, "Holy, Holy, Holy...Lord God Almighty." The lyrics soothed and encouraged, and the melody embraced the singers with peace. Bert and Alice stood shaking hands as the parishioners left the sanctuary.

CHAPTER SIXTEEN

Greg Hunt was going to pieces emotionally. Sixteen-year-old Cindy was ignoring house rules, defying every instruction he gave her. Cindy's homeroom teacher, Mrs. Tillison, had contacted Madeline. Cindy was failing in her studies, and wasn't turning in any homework. Greg felt helpless. He couldn't spank her; threats were his only weapon and inasmuch as there was no punishment, Cindy shrugged them off. The change had come gradually but started when she began attending a new-age church called Awakening. He and Madeline had visited it twice. Greg had asked a staff member for a copy of their doctrine. "We have no lingering doctrines," explained the woman. "Our doctrines are fluid, they change with the cultural needs of the people." No anchor, thought Greg... no guidelines.

Greg bundled his frustrations together and laid them at Bert's size eleven feet. Blamed Bert's orthodox intransigence for not keeping the young at Fair Haven. "If he'd only loosen up, Madeline...let a little glitter in, the kids would stay." Madeline said nothing. She knew her Cindy; a little pizza would never be enough. She kept her counsel. Greg wasn't ready for reasoning; he'd found a pigeon to blame, and he'd strip it of every feather to get even.

"The guy behind the pulpit's supposed to solve his parishioners' problems, right?" Greg declared stoutly to anyone willing to stop and listen to his inane palaver. Nor would Greg apply that illogical reasoning to any of his depositors who expected him to clean up their financial mess.

Bert spent Sunday afternoon in his study, a coffee mug his companion. He missed Alice. She'd headed to the airport right after service so that she could meet first thing in the morning with Carpenter about the OTR Foundation. As he drove her there, he was reluctant to let her go, and said so. "I'll be back in a couple of days, honey. I'll get the details ironed out. Our future plans for assisting traditional churches are tied up in this new foundation; and it has to meet all government and state regulations." Her plane took off. They would talk tonight after the evening service.

Weariness stood beside Bert as he gazed out of the office window watching his parishioners driving into the parking lot, unloading families and finding parking spaces. His plan now seemed ho hum, flat, mundane. He had nothing new to bring to the table; just plans for revamping traditional events that had worked in the past. "I'm tired," the preacher admitted to himself, "tired of fighting to keep church doctrine relevant; tired of schisms, tired of pretending to be upbeat, while fighting depression. Maybe it's time to retire. My generation is out of touch with 21ˢᵗ century culture. We've had our day...maybe it's time the new agers took center stage and dinosaurs moved to the wings."

Not since the death of Jenny had Bert felt so down, so defeated. He glanced at his watch; in 45 minutes he'd be standing before his people. "God help me," he prayed. "They're expecting me to tell them how to turn our church around. I've nothing new to tell them." No voice came from heaven in answer to his plea; no wind rattled the door, but a song penetrated his soul and gave Bert his answer. "Tell me the old, old, story of unseen things above; of Jesus and His glory, of Jesus and His love...tell me the story simply for I forget so soon." Bert's heart broke; tears coursed down his cheeks, fears and fatigue left his body. There would never be a new story; it was the old, old story of the Cross that changed men's hearts and brought them salvation.

There was a knock at the door, and Mike's head appeared. "Ready preacher? Your congregation awaits you." He grinned.

"Yeah, Mike, I'm ready. Got a good crowd tonight?"

Mike nodded. "Oh yeah, more than usual. Any particular song in mind, preacher?"

Bert answered easily. "How about 'Tell Me the Old, Old Story' just before you turn the service over to me?"

Mike nodded. "You got it! Haven't sung that oldie in quite a while." Mike left hurriedly; Sylvia's background music had just begun.

From the perch of his pulpit chair, Bert watched his congregation from a peripheral view. Anxiety was gone. Bert knew the direction the church would take, for the Spirit had guided him via that old gospel song. From the 1st century church, to the 21st century church, the theme of the gospel was Christ crucified. And it would continue to be until the trumpet sounded to take believers home. Preachers were called to preach the unsearchable love of God to men everywhere. Bert was girding up his loins, readying himself for the battle ahead. "How can the people hear without a preacher?" Paul the apostle had asked.

Mike finished the song service and turned to Bert, nodded, and left the platform for the front pew to Bert's left.

"Thanks Mike. You're a blessing, and I never tire of thanking God for you. Sylvia, I appreciate your loyalty to that piano." Voices said amen in agreement. Mike blushed.

A crystal glass of water sat at Bert's right on the podium. He raised it to the congregation in salute. They smiled and felt at ease. Their old pastor was back, even if his sartorial appearance made him seem aloof.

"I had an idea you'd be out in full force tonight." Laughter. "Figured you'd be interested in finding out what magic formula I had that can turn our church around. For months we've been a divided people; some members insisting we go progressive as many churches are doing. Other members are determined to remain traditional. To get started let's do a little reviewing of how the church began and for what purpose it came into being. The church began in the 1st century after Christ's resurrection and His ascension to heaven. The Holy Spirit, or the Comforter, descended from heaven and lighted upon a group of believers. Three thousand souls were saved that day, called Pentecost. The Spirit entered them and they became followers, disciples preaching the gospel of salvation. In twenty-one hundred years that message has not changed, but it has been muted by new age philosophies. This is what our division is all about: remain true to the gospel that has stood the test of time, or change it to mitigate 21st century ideologies." Bert stopped for a sip of water. He could feel tension growing in his congregation. He continued.

"While praying and seeking guidance from the Spirit, I found myself singing the words to the song you've just sung. Take a hymnal, and turn to page 424 and follow along with me as I read the second verse of that hymn."

Parishioners reached for hymnals and found the given page. Bert waited till the search ended; Sylvia was at the piano playing the lovely melody softly. Bert solemnly read the poignant words:

"Tell me the story slowly, that I may take it in. That wonderful redemption, God's remedy for sin. Tell me the story often, for I forget so soon; The early dew of morning has passed away at noon. Tell me the old, old story; tell me the old, old story; tell me the old, old story, of Jesus and His love."

It was a time of reflection; a time when the saved remembered hearing and reaching out to the Christ of the old, old story. Tears were wiped away; throats cleared and noses blown. Bert felt a peace in the sanctuary that had been missing. He prayed for wisdom as he spoke from his heart to his divided congregation.

"After much prayer and soul searching, I am convinced that instead of preaching to itching ears, my duty is to preach the old story; for we do forget too soon what we have been saved from and to whom we owe allegiance.

"We are working on plans to set up night classes for those interested in deeper study of the Bible. I'm in contact with some very grounded, mature Christians to help teach these classes. We need more, not less, of God's word; we may be the generation that sees Christ's return in the air. If so, we want to be able to lead people to Christ, before His second advent. I am also looking into the possibility of having tent revival meetings, and bringing in popular gospel musicians and quartets, duets, soloists, etc., to encourage the multitude to come to the meetings. Instead of shrinking our activities, we are going to flaunt our traditional foundation. For it is orthodox Christianity that still carries the unadulterated message of the Cross."

The congregation sat in rigid attention. Bert could not read their thoughts, but sensed their interest. He continued. "These plans will not satisfy those among us dedicated to changing with the times. To those of that mindset, I gently suggest you find another place of worship. I am dedicated to preaching the old story till God calls me home, or I am asked to resign. People are hurting; people need comforting. It is the gospel that satisfies the needs of men; and our church must provide it. Our city is called Safe Haven, our church Fair Haven, and we must be fair to the people by preaching the Word, that they may find the salvation we found when we became Christians." Bert reached for his water glass and took a long sip of water. How had his message resonated with the people? Would they ask for his resignation? He glanced at Mike but Mike was sitting, head bowed. Oh God, he prayed, what next?

Mrs. Massengill broke the silence. "We needed that message, preacher. I haven't forgotten the night I heard the old story and walked the aisle and accepted Christ as my Savior." She began to weep as she finished speaking. That's all it took. Without an invitation, people made their way to the altar, weeping, praying. Mike was on his knees, then was on the platform; Sylvia headed for the piano.

"I surrender all," Mike sang, while Sylvia, blinded by tears, played in accompaniment. It had been a long time since the people had displayed their emotions openly. Bert stayed on his knees beside the podium until the people resumed their seats and waited for closure.

"The Holy Spirit visited us tonight, no doubt about that," said a grateful Bert. "Pray for the plans we're working on. It is prayer that changes things, not our wisdom. Mike, would you please close our meeting in prayer?"

While Mike prayed, Bert exited from the choir door. He didn't want to interact with anyone; he needed his space. Mike found him peering out his office window, watching his congregation depart.

"Rather I not come in preacher?" Mike asked cautiously.

"No, come in. Better still, why not make us coffee? My spiritual high needs a shot of earthly caffeine to keep me grounded." He laughed at Mike's expression.

With coffee in hand, they went over the night's events. "It's been a long time since I've felt the Spirit's presence close at hand, preacher," said Mike. "I guess like so many I've taken my salvation for granted, paid little attention to its value. Like taking Ruthie for granted…never telling her how much I appreciate her and love her, till something happens to remind me that she's the most important person in my life and that I love her. Like that song says, we forget too soon what salvation really means to us." Mike sipped at his coffee.

"Yeah, Mike. I fretted over that message. Didn't know how I was going to say what I said, till the Spirit popped that hymn into my mind. The lyrics became my sounding board. I'm going preach what the people need, rather than what they think they want. I may find myself at the Greyhound bus terminal, Alice in hand, boarding for parts unknown, but I have to do what's right by God."

Mike nodded. He knew Bert; knew also brick walls looming ahead. But he was glad to be on the right path, no matter where God led them.

The phone was ringing when his key turned in the lock. "Alice," he exclaimed as he snatched up the land line in the family room.

"Where have you been Bert?" asked an upset Alice, with a bite in her tone. "I've been calling and calling. Is your cell turned off?"

"Honey, I'm sorry. Yeah, I turned it off when I got to church; our meeting was long, and Mike and I talked over coffee till round 9:45. I should have called before I left the office...." He trailed off.

She said more calmly, "I'm sorry, it's just been a long day, Bert." She stopped speaking and Bert could hear her sniffing.

"Awe honey, I feel like a heel for forgetting to turn on my cell. It won't happen again. When are you coming home sweetheart?"

"I've booked a late flight for Tuesday, so I'll be back in South Carolina around 11 p.m."

"I'll be at the airport," said a jubilant Bert.

"Tell me about tonight's meeting," Alice said expectantly.

For the next 45 minutes he replayed the evening's events. "Wish you could have seen that altar. It was filled with people weeping, praying, and getting right with God. We saw the Spirit in action tonight, honey. I missed you there but it went so well."

They wished each other good night and disconnected, both happy they would be in each other's company before long.

CHAPTER SEVENTEEN

Bert patted the place where Alice usually lay, happy in the thought that she'd be beside him again soon. The more Darlington Enterprises invaded their time, the more Bert began to feel a bit resentful. But when he reasoned that plans he'd laid out tonight would be funded by Darlington, his pique changed to gratitude. Can't have my cake and eat it too, he mused philosophically.

The sandman was just visiting an exhausted Bert, when his work was interrupted by the clang, clang, clang, of the landline beside Bert's bed. Groaning and grasping the instrument in the dark, he barely said "Pastor" when interrupted by a hysterical woman's voice.

"Pastor, pastor, we...I need help. Oh, oh, can you come over?" Her sobs grew louder.

It wasn't until a male voice in the background shouted, "Madeline, for pity's sake...you're making a fool of yourself; put the phone down," that he recognized the voice was Madeline Hunt's, and Greg was doing the scolding.

"Shut up, Greg!" shouted Madeline. "You hear me! Shut up. Instead of yelling at me for seeking help, you should be out scouring the neighborhood in search of her."

Oh, no, thought Bert; don't tell me I'm invited to settle a domestic quarrel.

"Pastor...sorry to bother you this late, but I'm desperate, and...."

"Madeline," soothed Bert, "I can't help you unless I know what the problem is. Something to do with Cindy?"

"Yes, yes, can you come over? It's too hard to explain over the phone."

"I'm on my way," said the designated healer of domestic problems.

He slipped a pair of slacks over pajama bottoms, pulled a sweatshirt over his top, grabbed car keys and wallet, and was on his way in less than 10 minutes. He looked like a homeless guy rather than a dignified preacher.

Every light was on downstairs when Bert drove into the Hunt's circular driveway. The huge oak door flung open as soon as he mounted the four stone steps. Madeline Hunt stood at the entrance in a tartan wool dressing gown looking almost deranged. As Bert stepped into the foyer, Madeline practically collapsed in his arms. Bert maneuvered her into the family room where Greg was sitting on a couch. Greg rose, but had nothing to say to Bert and looked with disgust at his wife. He walked to the glass patio doors and stood staring sentry-like into the dark, his back toward them.

Bert sat in a chair across from Madeline who was now safely on the couch. An uncomfortable quietness was present; the only sound was the clang of keys and coins Greg jangled in the pocket of his lounging robe. Bert turned him off and waited for Madeline to get hold of herself. She smiled weakly, thanked him for coming, began to cry, stopped and said, "So sorry, pastor, but I'm beside myself," lapsing again into tears.

"Madeline," said Bert quietly but firmly, "I'm doing no good just sitting here. Tell me why you called."

Greg muttered something inaudible. Bert ignored him.

Madeline nodded. "I'm not helping, carrying on like an idiot. But I've never had to deal with anything like this before." She grabbed a ball of sodden Kleenex and put it to her eyes.

Bert kept his cool and his mouth shut. She finally came to grips with her emotions and began. "I think Cindy's been kidnapped." She raised her eyes to see how he took that bit of news. A huge guffaw from Greg was ignored by Bert and Madeline.

"OK, that's a start. Now give me details."

"Well, Cindy left the house around 5:30 this evening, going to sleep over at Emma White's, and said she was going shopping at the mall in the morning. Of course, since there's no school tomorrow, I said yes. She asked me if I could lend her money. I gave her twenty dollars. She kissed my cheek, said she'd see me later, and off she went pulling her little suitcase, heading for Emma's house." Madeline dissolved into tears recounting the episode.

Bert knew he didn't have all the pieces to this puzzle; he'd have to dig. "You saw her walk? She didn't drive to Emma's? Was Cindy in the habit of walking to Emma's?"

"Hell, no! Cindy never walks anywhere!" inserted Cindy's father, still standing at the patio doors.

Before Madeline could bite back, Bert held up his hand and asked, "Cindy's car is here?"

Madeline nodded. "When I asked why she was walking, she said she needed the exercise. I didn't think anything about it, until now."

"If she's spending the night at Emma's, why do you think she's been kidnapped? I'm confused."

"But that's the problem, Bert...she's not there. Emma called around 9:00 wanting to speak to Cindy. I was flabbergasted. 'Isn't she with you?' I asked. Emma got flustered when I insisted on an answer. Then I heard Mrs. White ask Emma what was going on. I heard Emma mumble something, then Mrs. White got on the line. She soon straightened me out; she knew nothing about a sleepover, and no, Emma had no idea where Cindy was. Mrs. White sounded concerned, but miffed at the same time." Madeline looked embarrassed about Cindy's lie.

"She's partying," said Greg without leaving his post. "You can't believe a thing she says these days; probably partying with some low-life she knows we don't want her hanging out with. She'll be sneaking in when she thinks we're in bed asleep; mark my word."

Bert pressed on. "Have you checked with all her friends?"

Madeline nodded.

"Does she have a boyfriend?" Bert asked calmly, expecting fireworks from Greg.

"No!" said the uppity banker. "I told her she was too young to date."

Bert thought wryly how naive Greg was if he thought a teenager as outgoing as Cindy would forego the male population that easily. But Bert wasn't buying the kidnapping scenario. The Hunts lived the good life, but were far from having the kind of money kidnappers look for before stealing their kids. No; this sounded like partying off limits, or an assignation; but without a boyfriend?

He reiterated his question with adroitness. "You're sure there's no guy in the picture?"

143

"Not that we know of," confessed Madeline.

"Yeah, she does," said a young voice. Bert turned and saw Greg Jr. curled up in an armchair; he'd sneaked downstairs unnoticed.

"Greggie," scolded his mom, "you're supposed to be in bed. Now go; this conversation is not for your ears."

"Wait a minute, Madeline," said Bert holding up his hand. "Let's hear what the boy has to say. You say Cindy does have a boyfriend?" The younger Greg nodded. "How do you know?" Bert persisted.

Junior shrugged, then spoke without looking at any adult.

"I hear her on her cell every night talking and laughing. I can hardly get to sleep! She drools over him. I've seen them go off in his car after school."

"Do you know his name?" asked the pastor, ignoring the parents, zeroing in on the lad.

"Yeah, Terry. Terry Cotton. Cindy calls herself Mrs. Cotton and giggles," said her brother, his voice displaying the disgust of a normal ten-year-old dealing with the thought of relationships.

Greg Hunt left sentry duty, and joined Madeline. He was eager to hear what information Bert could extract from his son.

"What kind of car does Terry drive?" asked Bert casually.

"A beat-up Chevy."

"Know the color?"

"Yeah, a dirty dark green...he never washes it. Ugh."

"I don't suppose you know where he lives?"

Greg shook his head. "But he's in Cindy's yearbook."

"Get it," commanded his dad.

Greg Jr. ran off, but returned shortly with a well-worn yearbook and handed it to Bert. Bert flipped through the alphabetical index until he found Cotton, Terry, plus phone and address. Using his cell Bert dialed Cotton's landline. With the speaker phone on, they listened to the ring, ring, ring. Bert cringed when he saw that it was close to 1:00 a.m.

Finally a sleepy, gravely, irritated voice answered. "Yeah, who's calling at this ungodly hour?"

"Mr. Cotton?"

"Speaking. And you are...?"

"Pastor Davenport of Fair Haven Baptist Church. Sorry to disturb your sleep, but we're looking for a missing teenager, Cindy Hunt. We believe your son knows her. Has he seen her or know something that might help us locate her? Her folks are pretty upset."

"Oh yeah, yeah, I can imagine. Let me get his mother to wake him up, and ask. Hold on." With the open line, they heard Cotton say to his wife, "Get Terry awake, ask him if he knows anything about Cindy Hunt." Several moments passed, then came a female shriek; they heard Cotton address his wife; more talking. Crying was coming from Mrs. Cotton, with her husband trying to soothe her. He was back at the phone. "Terry's not in his room; his bed hasn't been slept in. What's going on?!"

Pastor Davenport had an idea.

"Mr. Cotton, I understand you must be upset. Cindy Hunt's been missing since 5:30 p.m. and I believe she could be with your Terry. From what I understand, they're pretty close. What is he driving?"

Cotton groaned at the thought of a runaway. "It's a 2000 dark green Chevy Impala," he answered.

"Do you know the license plate number?"

"Yeah, yeah I just got new tags for both our cars. There's only one digit different between his and mine." Cotton rattled off the license number. Bert wrote it down.

"Where do we go from here, preacher?" asked the angry father curtly.

"When I know something, believe me...you'll be the first to hear. Just pray for these two kids, Mr. Cotton. Teens have a way of zigging in the wrong direction at times."

"How well I'm acquainted with Terry's zigging and zagging. Don't think that boy'll ever learn to walk straight. Thanks, preacher. Sorry I've been short with you. Call me when you know anything, no matter what time it is."

With cell in hand, Bert scrolled till he found the right number. It seemed ages before a sleepy voice answered. "Captain Bennett here."

"Joe, it's Bert Davenport. I'm sorry to disturb you but we have a problem and I need your help."

"Of course. I know you wouldn't call in the middle of the night if it wasn't important. What is it?"

Bert replayed the scenario that was unfolding. "Runaways, you think?" asked Joe Bennett.

"Yeah, but to me, it has all the earmarks of an elopement, Joe. Crazy but my mind's telling me they're heading for Las Vegas. She going on 17 and he's 19. They can get married there...plenty of charlatans'll tie a knot for a few bucks."

Greg Hunt stiffened, caught his breath, and sat down heavily on the couch. He listened open-mouthed at the conversation between Pastor and the lawman. Was his Cindy capable of pulling this kind of stunt? He cradled his head in his hands, and moaned quietly.

Madeline covered her mouth with her hands to keep from sobbing. Young Greg snickered and sank deeper into the armchair.

Bert gave Captain Bennett details about the car and about the two teens involved. "My instinct tells me they're probably in some rest area, getting some sleep. Haven't much money, so I doubt they could afford to stay anywhere. It'll be a while before they get anywhere near Las Vegas."

"I'll be here till I hear from you, Captain. You know my number." He recited the number to reach the Cotton family, then looked at Greg. Greg recited both cell and landline numbers, and Bert passed them to Captain Bennett. "Thanks Cap, as I said, I owe you." Bert laughed at Bennett's repartee. "Yeah, yeah, I know...but I really will make good on those IOUs. Thanks again." Bert closed his cell.

Erie silence followed the phone conversation. Greg broke the tension, saying quietly, "Madeline, why don't you fix coffee for Pastor, he could probably use a cup. So could I. And Greg, you need to head back to bed right now, young man."

Greg reluctantly obeyed; Madeline was on her feet. "For goodness sake. I'm losing my manners along with my mind." She was on her way to the kitchen murmuring, "Sorry, Pastor."

Greg wanted to apologize for messing up the church's bank account, but now wasn't the time. They sat in silence until Madeline returned with coffee and cookies. Greg rose, taking the tray from her and placing it on the coffee table, murmuring, "Looks good, honey."

"Looks great, Madeline. I confess I'm a bit hungry and in need of caffeine." At their request, Bert thanked God for the food and spent a few minutes invoking God's help in finding the young people. A peace fell over them. Conversation turned to the plans Bert had laid out for the church.

Greg, without rancor, commented, "It's an ambition plan, Pastor. I have an idea it'll catch on with our people; maybe challenge our youth." Greg was reaching out to Bert, was grateful for his wisdom and help in dealing with Cindy's disappearance. He cringed when he thought of Cindy married at 16, her life impacted forever by her decisions that day. Greg had never considered Bert anything but a dull minister dishing out sermons. Now he recognized the depth of experience Bert had developed through years of counseling parishioners. Who among them had had the opportunity, as they had tonight, of seeing this side of their pastor?

Bert was pleased to hear this coming from Hunt. He could feel the shift in Greg's attitude toward him, and knew it meant a change in the tense relationship between them.

Coffee saturated silence, accompanied by the Sandman, meant sleep descended on the exhausted trio. They dozed, Madeline on the couch, Greg in his leather recliner, Bert on the upholstered Lazy boy.

The phone rang like a fire alarm. Bert sat upright; Greg jerked his recliner into sitting position. Madeline looked scared to death. "Why don't you answer it, Pastor, it's probably..."

Bert nodded, picked up the phone, and punched the speakerphone option. "Hello?"

"Well, padre...we got 'em. They're on their way home right now. They were spotted at a rest area near Conyers, Georgia. She was asleep in the backseat; he was dozing up front. They were scared to death when the officers shone flashlights into the car. Thought they were going to be killed by robbers. That pair won't be running away anytime soon, and if they do...it'll be with other partners. I think they'd had a lovers' quarrel. The officers told them they needed to head home, and they didn't argue. Tell their folks they're OK, be home when the miles are eaten up. It's been one exciting night, but hey, I'm too old for this. I'm off to bed. G'night." He was gone in the middle of Bert's effusive thanks.

Bert dialed the number that was scrawled on the notepad on the coffee table and gave Mr. Cotton the good news. "Thanks preacher...thanks again. What a night it must have been for that girl's parents, too."

Bert rose to his feet, stretched stiff limbs, and reached for his jacket. Like Joe, he was getting too old for midnight forays. He envisioned his bed, and longed to be in it. Madeline had stopped crying and was smiling from ear to ear. "Bert what would we have done without your sixth sense coming to the rescue? I've never been happier. Tomorrow I'm taking Cindy to the mall and buying her the best outfit she's ever had."

Bert stopped midway into his jacket sleeve, and stared at her. "Madeline, why on earth would you want to reward her for deceiving you and putting your family through this agony? If you reward her, she won't think twice about pulling a stunt like this again. And next time, it might not end without irreversible damage." Bert finished zipping his jacket and headed for the front door. Greg walked beside him.

Madeline followed, stammering, "I just felt so relieved, I wanted to buy something. I guess I wasn't thinking straight."

"If you want to buy something, take your son to the mall and treat him. He actually contributed to the solution. Or buy yourself a new pair of shoes or something, but do not reward Cindy; that's my personal counsel."

At the door, Greg thanked Bert profusely. "Don't know where we'd be right now if you hadn't come to our rescue. I've got things to straighten out with you...can we meet?"

"Sure thing, Greg. Just call the office and we'll figure out a good time."

A penitent Madeline asked, "If you were in our shoes, Bert, what would you do if it were your daughter?"

"I would take her car keys and tell her she can get them back when her attitude changes and she obeys house rules."

Madeline frowned. "How would she get to school?"

"Is the school bus not running?"

"Yes, but..."

"There's you answer; let her ride the bus."

Madeline shuddered. "She'll be unbearable to live with if we take her keys."

"Well, how is it living with her now?" asked Bert. "Can you really continue to let this kind of behavior go without repercussion? I would also suggest that you consider no longer paying for her cell phone. That'll get her attention. It won't be easy, Madeline. But waiting here for hours wasn't easy on you, was it? My advice has merit–I've dished it out many times, and it works."

After a short prayer with the couple, Bert headed out of the Hunt's front door and was home shortly. In no time, he was fast asleep, dreaming of Alice.

By morning, a pair of police officers brought a tired, grumpy Cindy Hunt home to her parents. Greg was informed that he had to come to the station later in the day to sign paperwork about the incident. Greg assured them that he'd be there; the police departed.

Cindy Hunt stared at her parents. If she had imagined a loving welcome, her expectations expired the moment she looked at them. Madeline just stared at her; Greg said quietly, "Go get some rest and we'll talk later in the morning. Where are your car keys?"

She looked surprised, but shrugged and dug into her purse. She handed her dad the set of keys. Greg pocketed them and said, "Thank you. You won't be needing them until I determine how well you've adjusted to the rules of this household. Now, go to bed."

Cindy's eyes went from tired to shocked; her mouth fell open in utter disbelief. She sputtered and shouted angrily, "You can't take my car keys. I need those! How dare you? I never should have turned around! This is insane!"

"Go to bed, Cindy," said Greg, holding his fury at bay. He and Madeline headed upstairs.

"Mom! You can't let him treat me like this! Mom!" she shouted after them, volume rising with each word. Greg and Madeline continued climbing the stairs. Cindy came to the foot of the stairs and screamed after them. "Dad, you're a prick and a hypocrite and I hate you! You can't just take my car! Mom! You know he's a freaking jerk and you're staying with him! If you're so religious why're you running that boring prick of a preacher out of town? You're nothing but a freaking fraud! I'm gonna tell the whole town you molested me. You're going to be sorry you ever took my keys!"

By the time she finished her thought, Greg was beside her, pointing an index finger in her face. "You go right ahead young lady and lie to the town. We'll help you pack because they'll pull you right out of here. But don't take anything of value with you, 'cause you might run into some nasty characters while you're waiting for a nice foster home to open up."

Cindy's bravado melted like marshmallows over fire, but Greg went on. "If you falsely accuse me of something terrible, you can kiss your car goodbye for good because I'll lose my job, and you'll lose all the comforts my job gives you. You better think long and hard before you go down that road. Now...go to bed!"

Greg went back up the steps, closing the bedroom door with a decisive click. Cindy stared after them and yelled obscenities at her father's retreating figure. She stamped her feet and headed for the kitchen, screaming in frustration.

After a few minutes with no one to complain to, Cindy stomped up the stairs, thought better of kicking their door, sighed, and went to her room, slamming the door for effect. She didn't even bother to change out of her clothes; she flung herself into bed, fuming helplessly at the dilemma she found herself in. Exhausted but too angry to sleep, Cindy lay mouthing oaths she imagined throwing at her dad next time she saw him. At no time did she think to blame herself for her predicament.

She couldn't believe her folks hadn't welcomed her home with tears and kisses. What had gotten into her dad? How dare he take away her car? He had never even warned her about that possibility before.

Cindy was secretly glad to be home, grateful to have been rescued before getting to Las Vegas. Ugh...the thought of marrying Terry now gave her the creeps. What had she ever seen in him anyway? What a leach! He'd come with enough money to fill the gas tank once. Period. Her money bought food and gas beyond that. He wasn't even embarrassed to take HER money. Thank goodness they didn't stay in some sleazy motel; that would have been even more awkward!

Meanwhile, behind the closed door of the bedroom, Madeline was leaning against the headboard of their bed, bedclothes wrapped tightly round her, staring into nothingness, when Greg finally finished in the bathroom and came toward the bed.

"Honey," he said soothingly, looking at her. "She's just letting off steam; probably so tired she doesn't know what's she's saying." Madeline didn't move, just kept staring into space. Greg wondered if she'd heard him. He repeated himself but still no response. Panic struck him; wasn't she way too young to have a stroke?!

Cindy heard her dad run down the stairs; heard him talking wildly to someone. Curious, she opened her door and listened. Dad was upset, his voice panicky. It couldn't be about her; she was home.

"Sam! I don't know what to do. Maddie's acting strange, like a zombie; she's not answering me at all. I'm afraid she's had a stroke. Can you come or should I call 911, and get her to emergency?" Pause, pause, then, "Yeah... and you can call from here...yeah, OK." Another pause. "Yeah she got really upset tonight over a stunt Cindy pulled. I'll fill you in when you get here. Please Sam, hurry!"

Cindy realized her dad was crying! She closed her door, leaned against it, and slid to the floor. She heard Greg run up the stairs and say something to her mom, but she heard nothing from her mom. Greg was saying, "Hang in honey, everything's OK. Here, take a drink of water...please, Maddie just a little sip!"

This is all my fault! thought Cindy. What if something terrible happened to her mom, and the last words she heard were those awful hate-filled words? Cindy had never used that kind of language before. She wondered how it had suddenly come out of her mouth. A verse from Sunday school surfaced in her mind: "Out of the heart the mouth speaketh." Kids she hung around with thought foul language was normal and cool; it made them feel powerful. But Cindy didn't talk like that, until today.

Dr. Sam Armstrong was at his sister's side in less than 10 minutes. He checked her pupils, her pulse, her breathing, and quickly ruled out a stroke. But Madeline's aphonic state continued. "Maddie, it's your little brother. Your kids need you, Maddie, we all do. Come on, fight through the fog. Squeeze my hand, wake up."

They waited, watching, until she moved her hand slightly and blinked. Sam was professionally detached, but Greg was on his knees, face full of concern as he worked to hold back tears. He took her hand, kissed it, and said "Honey, I love you so much, I need you to come back to me; C'mon babe, look at me." Greg rubbed his face to her hand, praying silently.

Finally, after what seemed an eternity but was only a minute, Madeline Hunt moved her head and looked around her. She looked at Greg, then noticed her brother. "What are you doing here Sam?" she asked softly. "Is everything OK?" She looked at Greg still on his knees. "What's going on—is Greggie OK?" Greg turned away from them to hide tears that were coursing down his cheeks.

"Oh God," he breathed. "Oh God, thank You, thank You. I don't deserve this mercy."

Madeline was moving to get out of bed. "What time is it?" she asked.

"6:30 Monday morning," answered Dr. Sam.

"I need some coffee," she announced. "Give me a minute and I'll fix some for us."

Greg started to protest but Sam shook his head, and mouthed, "Let her!"

Cindy watched till her uncle left the house; her mom didn't go with him. Was that a good sign or a bad one, she wondered. She crept to the top of the stairs where she could hear what was going on. She heard her mom say something; then heard her dad laugh. Cindy sighed with relief. Tears were running down her cheeks when she sneaked back into her bedroom, closing the door softly. Her mom was OK. Relief sent her to her knees, thanking God for her mom's recovery. She crept under the covers and exhaustion put her to sleep.

It was 1:30 p.m. when the noise under her window woke Cindy. Glancing out her bedroom window, she saw her mom, dad and her brother getting into the family car. They were all smiles. Last night's anger resurfaced; scare over her mother was gone, replaced with resentment at not being included in the family's happiness. They aren't even worried about me, she thought to herself. She showered before heading to the kitchen for food. She ate cold cereal and dialed Emma's cell.

"Hi Emma, can you come over? I'm alone, my family just took off without me." She laughed shakily.

When Emma answered it was in a whisper. "Cindy, I can't talk to you anymore, or hang out with you. My mom's upset about you lying about being here. If I contact you they're going to take my cell away. So, please don't call me."

A voice behind Emma sent Cindy back on her heels. "If that's Cindy, you better hang up. You know what your father said last night." Emma's cell went dead. Cindy stared at the little red case in her hand. Her social life had just come to a grinding halt; what Emma had said would be passed around to her peers and she'd be shut out. This felt worse than death.

Panic followed that thought. Her wheels gone; how was she going to get to school in the morning? She called Ruby Connors. She didn't like her much, but she'd be good for a ride. After two rings a voice came through.

"Cindy! You're the last person I expected to hear from today!"

"Ruby, hey, can you give me a ride to school in the morning? I have no car for right now."

"Wow, Cindy, I heard all about your elopement! When'd you get home? Lose your wheels because you were a naughty girl?" Her laugh was crueler than her words. "Emma already told me, guess you're off her guest list now!" Ruby was barely taking a breath between the boasts and insults.

Cindy, sick of her hubris, shut off the call without responding. She dreaded school tomorrow. She'd have to ride the school bus. She'd be the laughing stock of the school...her best friend Emma, no longer her friend—Ruby had confirmed that. She had never been on the negative side of peer pressure; now she'd be ridiculed unmercifully! On top of that, her parents were angry with her; her mom had been sick enough to call in Uncle Sam. Oh God, she moaned, get me out of this mess, please.

CHAPTER EIGHTEEN

Alice called when Bert had reached his office. "How is your day going, honey?" she asked.

"Just fine now, but I miss you like crazy. You aren't going to believe the night I had last night! God's working on Greg Hunt, big time."

"Oh my, what happened?" asked Alice.

Bert gave her a short version of Cindy Hunt's interrupted elopement and his night vigil with the family.

"My word," said Alice. "Who'd have thought that Greg would be brought to his knees in such a fashion? It's a miracle. Wonder how this is going to play out with his crowd at church? He's going to have to eat crow... but I think he's the kind of guy who'll do it."

"Yeah, honey. Never thought I'd see Greg so humbled. But kids can do that to you...scare you to death. I'll wager Cindy's going to have a time at school. Her friends will suddenly become her enemies. A page out of Job—his friends thought up things to throw at him. Peers turn savage when the one who once was kingpin loses their crown. But I believe we're seeing the last of Hunt's war against me, or I'm no judge of men, but we'll see. I'll see you tomorrow, right, darling?"

"Yes, I think I've got everything in motion here. The foundation will meet all the requirements, thanks to David's determination to follow every jot and tittle of the law. Soon we'll be ready to print brochures and application forms. David said he'd see that news of the OTR Foundation gets around. He suggested that we set up a mediator to handle the first phase of application, before it gets to the foundation board. I had a chance to think about it, and I think Rev. Butler would be perfect for the job. So, what do you think? I'm really surprised by David's enthusiasm for the foundation. He's actually anxious to see it in action."

Bert felt a tinge of jealousy when Alice talked about David Carpenter. He was a good looking guy, and his interest in Alice was obvious. If she hadn't married me, thought Bert sullenly, David would have chased her till he married her. "But she married YOU," an inner voice scolded, "So get over it!" Bert shook his head at his foolishness, and told jealousy to take a hike.

Bert gathered his thoughts enough to finally answer, "Yes, Rev. Butler would be perfect for the job! I'll give him a call this afternoon."

Tuesday morning had arrived, and it seemed that every eye watched her climb onto the school bus, take a seat in the back, and attempt to be invisible as the bus made its rounds.

"Aww poor Cindy, no car?" asked a classmate. Cells had been working overtime, and Emma White had made sure no secrets remained. Catcalls and innuendoes floated like hot air balloons around the bus.

The bus driver finally called a halt to the verbal abuse when she realized what was going on. "Keep your mouths shut, if you can't say something nice," she warned.

Cindy's entrance into her first hour caused a ripple through the class. Talking ceased, and noisy whispering began spiraling out of control, until Mrs. Tillison entered the classroom. Cindy, trying hard to hold back tears, was grateful for the formidable teacher's presence. Students returned to their seats; academia was in session, and flaying their victim was put on hold.

Terry Cotton was faring much, much better. His friends were egging him on to tell about the elopement. Terry, enjoying the limelight, embellished the weekend with lurid untruths. By lunchtime, Cindy's character was tarnished, shredded, and gutted. Mrs. Tillison, as did most faculty members, knew about the aborted elopement. When Tillison heard from a male teacher the salacious tidbits Terry was dishing out, she trekked to the principal's office to put a stop to it.

Terry sat on a hard chair in Principal Shelby's office. His boastings mocked him as he watched a video of himself, caught on a fellow student's cell phone, spinning tales about his night with Cindy Hunt. The recording nailed him.

"So, Mr. Cotton," said Stanley Shelby, "have you forgotten that you're a guest in this school, and 19? A year ago you dropped out of school. After a few months you were back begging to be allowed to finish high school. You were 18 when you dropped out. By law the system was under no obligation to educate you. I felt sorry for you, and I allowed you to return to finish out your last year, which will end in seven weeks. According to this video, you've been boasting and bragging to your classmates about a so-called elopement, and spreading scurrilous rumors about one of my students. I should tell you to clean out your desk and never return to this school." Shelby paused for effect. "Because I believe in the power of education, I will let you remain. But if you spread any more gossip or your buddies keep harassing this student, you will be shown the door—whether it's seven weeks or one week before graduation. Do I make myself clear?"

A cowed Terry hung his head and nodded vigorously. "Dismissed," said the principal. Terry rose and made for the door. Before he reached his exit, the principal added, "You should be praying that Mr. Hunt doesn't take you to court for enticing his 16-year-old daughter to run away with a 19-year-old man. Think about that, Mr. Cotton." Terry knew he could keep his own mouth shut, but getting some of the guys he told to shut up would be a herculean task. What a mess, he thought.

Mrs. Tillison handed Cindy a thick manila envelope as she was leaving class that afternoon. "Your makeup homework, Cindy," she said quietly. Cindy winced at the size of the neglected homework.

"I'll get right on it Mrs. Tillison," said a subdued Cindy.

She stood at the rear of the bus line, dreading the ride home. She couldn't take another barrage of ugly remarks and dirty innuendoes. A car pulled curbside, and a voice called "Cindy!"

She bent down and recognized the driver.

"Want a ride?" shouted Lisa Brown. Without answering, Cindy opened the passenger door and slid into the shabby Ford Escort. Lisa pulled away from the curb as the bus stopped at the line of kids.

Cindy shuddered. "Boy, Lisa, you'll never know how much I appreciate this. I was dreading that bus ride home." She looked over at the driver.

Lisa said nothing, but nodded. Lisa knew how she'd felt; having had to ride the bus when her car had been taken away had been miserable. She liked Cindy Hunt, but no longer aspired to be one of Cindy's circle. Trying to be part of the popular crowd had caused Lisa to change personality and lose her car. With help from Pastor, she'd set her own goals and self-esteem now came from achievements, not relationships.

As they distanced themselves from the school, Cindy relaxed a bit, and her pent-up emotions gave way. Tears ran down her cheeks, and although she kept her head turned, Lisa knew she was crying. Even though they weren't close friends, Lisa felt a pang of compassion for Cindy. She knew Cindy would have more to contend with because Cindy had worn the crown, set the pattern copied by her acolytes from hair style to perky mannerisms. Lisa was used to living outside the box; her family shopped at Goodwill, and horror of horrors...she had a redneck for a father, who worked in a lumber mill.

Lisa maneuvered the car through the streets, headed for Cindy's house. She marveled at the fickleness of peers who clamored for Cindy's attention, but could turn on her on a dime. Where were the classmates Cindy went to church with? Lisa drew to the curb in front of the Hunt's lovely home. She turned to Cindy, who was wiping her eyes and looking miserable.

"This too shall pass, Cindy," Lisa Brown said prosaically. "Nothing remains the same. Something else will come along, and they'll move on to other news...that's how it works."

Cindy shook her head. "No, no, I'm never going back to school, to wait for that to happen. I'll get a tutor...I'll do something!"

Lisa looked at her coldly. "You think you're the only one that's been trashed by peers? I've endured what you had today ever since junior high. I'm a zero, a nothing. Only good for making fun of when things get dull. I was desperate until I went to see Pastor Davenport. He gave me advice that I use to this day."

Cindy reddened; she'd been one who had joked about Lisa's clothes; especially the day Lisa came to school wearing a skirt Cindy's mom had donated to the church's clothes closet.

In spite of herself, Cindy asked, "What did Pastor tell you?" She was reluctant to leave the car and face her dad, after her horrible behavior the day before.

"He told me that life's one problem after another. The weak run, the strong stay and fight back, but not by using their own power. That's a waste of time and energy. You overcome by leaning on God, and turning wasteful anger into productive fuel. You set goals and use that fuel to reach new heights. He reminded me of the verse, 'I can do all things through Christ which strengtheneth me.' Don't waste time getting even. Vengeance is God's, and He takes care of His own."

Lisa paused, and when she sensed Cindy was listening, continued. "Now, instead of dwelling on anger, I use my emotion to get something done I'd put aside. People at school have stopped bothering me. They can't figure me out. I'm oblivious to their snide remarks, and there's no fun in harassing a dead horse...so their pleasure of torment is gone. It wasn't easy to ignore them at first, but now I pity them."

Cindy picked up her homework envelope and reached for the door handle. Before getting out she turned to Lisa. "Do you think it would work for me...you know...ignoring their gossip without screaming back at them?"

"It's up to you, but it sure beats running from school and adding more fuel to the rumors. But it takes resolve. I prayed long and hard before I decided to give the preacher's advice a try. I had to bite my tongue and constantly pray for God to keep me above the fray. Once I'd found that discipline, it got easier; and before long, I wasn't aware of my agitators because I was so focused on what I was accomplishing. Prayer is where the power lies. You know how to pray...so use that power. What do you have to lose?"

Cindy blushed; she'd ceased thinking prayer was effective until the scare over her mom sent her to her knees. Lisa was speaking truth, and Cindy recognized it.

"Lisa, you know the Bible says we're to confess our sins, and until we do God doesn't hear us. Right?" Lisa nodded.

"Well, I was horrible to my parents when they took my car keys, and that was after lying to them and taking off with a guy. We're not speaking. I need to apologize. I'm ashamed of how I acted. What should I do to make amends?"

"What you just said is what they need to hear. Tell your mom and dad you're sorry for the things you said and did, and ask them to forgive you. Do it right away, before you tackle your school problems."

Cindy nodded, picked up her homework, pushed open the car door, and slid out. She bent forward as she closed the door. "You've given me more than a ride home, Lisa. You've given me friendship and counseling I'm going to put into action. Thanks for the ride. Maybe Friday night we could take in a movie."

Lisa shook her head. "I'm sorry, it sounds great but I can't. I'm part of the planning committee for our teens. We're having teens from other churches join us for a barbecue and marshmallow roast after our youth meeting Friday night. You should come! Think about it." She didn't give Cindy time to reply, just waved and drove off. Cindy watched her go and had newfound respect for her. Lisa's the real deal, Cindy thought. Guilt made her grimace when she thought how often she'd joined in with the other girls to make life miserable for Lisa Brown.

Cindy started for the front door when Madeline, bringing Greggie home from school, turned into the driveway. Cindy followed them into the house via the garage.

CHAPTER NINETEEN

Ministerial conventions are conundrums. They bring out the best and the worst in preachers. A subtle caste system exists among the clergy. The Catholic church defines caste with titles: Cardinals, Bishops, Priests. Protestants' subtle pecking order is couched in size: large church; medium church; small church; and weighed and labeled according to Sunday School attendance and size of offerings. God may not be a respecter of people, but the clergy certainly is. In spite of disparity among the brethren, ministers come long distances, not only for a change in scenery, but to exchange anecdotes about what's going on in their church beside marrying, burying, and encouraging their sheep.

Good preaching from preachers who've overcome, and preachers who've felt the hand of God in a desperate situation, all help feed the flagging spirits of some ministers who feel like throwing in the towel, some with their resignation letter already tucked away in their office desks. While "Faith is the substance of things hoped for," there comes a time when men of the cloth need a little "evidence of things not seen." This was one conference that every minister would attend for a lifeline of hope extended to them.

"We're hosting the ministerial conference," Bert had announced weeks before the event. That's all it took. Fair Haven parishioners became a bevy of committees: food, drinks, décor, and accommodations for pastors and wives eschewing hotel expenses. The parishioners were anxious to show off the new roof, the new parking lot, and the maroon carpeting in the sanctuary.

Bert's people outdid themselves, making him proud, and everything was ready when the date arrived.

Dr. Ivo Hinton was president of the convention that year. Bert had clued him in weeks before regarding the new foundation he'd be introducing. An excited Hinton wanted chapter and verse. "Is the foundation legit? Is there any chance this is a scam? C'mon Bert, you've gotta know more than you're telling."

Bert was adamant; stuck to the narrative he and Alice had decided on. "I'm telling you all I can tell, Ivo. The foundation's donors want anonymity. It's a small price to pay for the grant money."

Hinton shrugged off irritation but had to concede anonymity was a reasonable trade off. He figured he'd have his computer-savvy son dig up additional information. His son tried, but failed; everything was blocked about the funding of OTR Foundation.

Tuesday afternoon, Hinton stood behind Bert's pulpit, looking the part of a leader. "Sorry to take up preaching time, but I think you're going to want to hear what I have to tell you." He grinned, and got on with it. He was speaking to an all-male audience; wives had done their duty listening to morning sermons and had taken off for the mall.

He noticed that he had the attention of nearly everyone in the room. "I can't divulge the name of the bird that brought this manna to my attention, but take my word for it...he's above reproach where truth is concerned." Hinton launched into his narrative. A new foundation had just been established called OTR (Old Time Religion). Its purpose for existing was to undergird traditional churches struggling to keep from closing their doors because of lack of funds. "The foundation is well endowed, is properly vetted via government legal standards," explained Hinton. "Before you ask, no, this is not a scam. I understand that one church has already applied and is now a beneficiary of their generosity."

Preachers were sitting up straighter and leaning closer to the speaker. Several arms shot up with questions. Hinton held up his hand. "We'll get to your questions in a moment."

Some grumblings, but common sense prevailed, and the ministers relaxed, waiting for more information. "So that you have complete details about the foundation, we have brochures and application packets we'll pass out in a few moments. I do know they are located in New York City. Their goal is to further orthodox Christianity by helping churches that are struggling against the deluge of liberal social gospel and progressivism.

In order to get help, the pastor of a traditional church must fill out an application form and submit it to a mediator, who in turn screens it. It is either accepted and sent on to New York, or denied and returned to the sender."

"Could I have a couple of you grab the brochures and application forms and pass them to your colleagues? Read them and then we'll answer questions." Volunteers got the job done in quick time. Silence fell as the ministers digested the printed words that spelled hope for their desperate situation. "Everyone get a copy of each?" Heads nodded.

There was silence except for the turning of pages. Bert, viewing from a vantage point near the back, watched as the men read eagerly their "evidence of things not seen." When most heads rose to meet his eyes, Hinton nodded and said, "Now, your questions. Pastor Jeffries, you first."

"Do we commit our church property in any way for grant money?"

"No Brother Jeffries, if you qualify for a grant, there is no property requirement. The foundation is not interested in acquiring church properties."

"What about a reverse mortgage?" asked a still skeptical Jeffries.

"Answer's the same," replied Hinton. "Once the money's dispersed... it's the church's."

"This application form is pretty detailed, Bro. Hinton. A man bears his soul when he answers these questions." Rev. Joe Clark waited for an answer.

"You're exactly right, Bro. Clark. It will be on the strength of how you answer those questions, whether you qualify for grant money or not. The Foundation donors want to help orthodox Christian pastors, not pretenders or progressive-leaning preachers. The application is subtle; it reveals a man's inner being. When I filed my application, I had to do some soul searching before answering some questions. When I completed the form, I knew without any equivocation what my core beliefs were, and that I could never preach any gospel but the gospel of Christ. This Foundation will not give a dime to pastors that could be swayed from the straight and narrow."

"I take it then," said Rev. Stan Ratcliff, "that acceptance or rejection is predicated on our answers?"

Hinton nodded. "You got it. And if you fudge and get a grant, when you apply for an additional grant, if you've accomplished nothing but paid bills with the first, your request will be denied."

"What about the guy who looks over our applications and decides whether to send them to New York or back to us. Supposing he doesn't like us...you know..."

Hinton shook his head. "The mediator is a retired pastor who has spent years in service to his church without swaying from the Gospel message. He was once in your shoes and knows exactly what you're going through. I think you will find him more than fair in his assessment of the paperwork you fill out. Any other questions?"

"Is this a onetime grant, Dr. Hinton, or can we apply for more later?"

"As I think I said, you can, but you will have to have some great plans in place. They are interested in helping churches grow. Be bold in stating your aspirations for growth. If you are making headway with your goal, you will get additional help. The Foundation is interested in progress related to the goals you delineate on your application form. They don't expect miracles; they're aware of what's going on in churches. But they want to see that you are pursuing your goal. If you are, when you reapply you will probably qualify for another grant. They want to have this money result in souls being added to the Kingdom."

Questions came to a stop when a female voice announced, "Dr. Hinton, dinner is served in the fellowship hall." The ministers made their way to tables where their wives were seated, many in excited conversation with one another about their plans to apply for grants.

At their final meal, Dr. Hinton stood at the head of the table and addressed Bert. "Brother Davenport, I speak for the brethren. We have been treated royally by your wonderful people. We have lacked for nothing physically nor spiritually. Please express our deepest thanks to your flock for making this one of the most memorable conventions we've had in a long, long time. God bless you and the visions you have for the future of your church." All the people rose, if somewhat awkwardly from the tables, and applauded Bert and his congregation vigorously.

Hinton asked Bert to pray. Bert nodded. "We're a blessed people, Lord, because we know You as our Father, our Creator, and our Redeemer.

Endow these brethren with vision and strength to be bold and tackle their goals. Return them safely to their pulpits, in Jesus' name we pray. Amen."

The ministers were reluctant to leave; they stood chatting in the parking lot, exchanging views, hopes, and visions of the future should this OTR Foundation live up to its promises. Wives eventually broke in with gentle but firm voices, cognizant of the distance some had to drive to get back home. Wives had a way of spoiling wool gathering.

"Well," said Ivo Hinton as they approached his car, "looks like we're the last to leave." He opened the passenger door for his wife; Miriam slid in. Standing at the driver's door, he put out his hand to Bert. "Been the most momentous meeting I've attended since my early days in the ministry. Heaven really did come down." He glanced at Bert solemnly. "What d'you think; will many send in applications? Do you think I convinced them it's worth a try?"

"I don't know Ivo. Depends on how desperate their situation is and if they figure they've nothing to lose but a postage stamp. You did an excellent job in explaining OTR; you convinced me it was legit. Preachers on the verge of retiring may not bother, and leave it up to their successor. But on the other side of the coin, preachers ready to resign may take heart, fill in the application, and catch a new vision. Remember, Ivo, we men of the cloth need to let the Holy Spirit be our guide. So we'll have to wait and see. The younger men will be more apt to reach out than the older ones. I see young preachers applying, confident that they'll be able to get a grant regardless of qualifications delineated in the application form. Figure their glib pen will override any postmodern bent they try to hide. I wouldn't want to bet, but I've an idea their application will be denied. As you pointed out...the application is like a scalpel. The foundation is not run by fools. It is adamant on this score: it will not fund new age ideologies."

"What are your plans, Bert?"

"Next week all media outlets will carry ads about our free Bible studies that will be taught by solid, biblically grounded theologians. All adults regardless of church affiliation are welcome to attend. We're posting on social media our sermon titles for the coming weeks. 'ARE YOU READY TO MEET GOD?,' 'WILL YOU BE LEFT BEHIND AT THE RAPTURE?,' and 'ARE WE LIVING IN THE LAST DAYS?'"

Hinton looked at Bert and shook his head. "Well bully for you my brother clergyman. That's what I call being bold for Christ. Go big or go home, right?!" He laughed uproariously and slid into the driver's seat at the summons of his wife.

"Ivo, we've got to get home!"

Hinton leaned out the window to catch Bert's last remarks. "Later we're going to launch a tent revival." Bert laughed at the look of shock on Hinton's face before he pressed the button and the driver's window slid to a close. Bert watched as their car drove slowly from the parking lot, turned left, and merged with road traffic. He went in search of Alice.

Seated in the family room later that evening, they rested with his arms around her as they replayed the events of the week. "Great, great convention," said Bert sighing.

Alice, leaning against his shoulder, agreed. "It was one convention that didn't bore me," she confessed. "I'd like to do something to thank the members who worked tirelessly to make it great, but don't know the best way to do that."

"What about serving coffee and donuts for the congregation after Sunday night's service? That way we'd be recognizing those who worked hard, without missing anyone."

"Oh I like it! That's a great idea. I'll order donuts in the morning for Sunday evening. That's a perfect idea, Bert." She kissed him happily. He returned the kiss gratefully.

"Alice, I'd better get word to John that the church isn't paying for the donuts." They laughed in unison.

Greg caught her unaware when he entered the kitchen; she was rummaging through the fridge. Without hesitation he said, "C'mon Cindy, let's go to IHOP for breakfast. We need to talk."

Cindy shrugged. "Let me get my jacket and purse, Dad." Retrieving both she followed Greg to the car. He drove to the IHOP, a place he seldom ate at. Inside the half-full restaurant, they were seated in a booth and given menus. Ordering breakfast took the edge off the awkwardness of the moment. When the waitress left, embarrassment sat between them. Cindy tried hard to avoid eye contact with her dad.

"We're here to get a few things straight," Greg said quietly, leaning a little forward to be heard. "First, this impasse between you and the family ends here and now." He took a sip of water and looked at her, but there was no eye contact. "I'm making it easy for you to bridge the gap by telling you that your mom and I love you, and have forgiven your runaway stunt." He wouldn't say the word elopement...too suggestive...too upsetting. "Your vulgar language I forgive. I know it was said in anger, but that does not excuse its ignorance. It has no place in our household. You will refrain from ever using it again, or there will be consequences. Understand?"

Greg waited. Cindy finished sipping water, and nodded.

"We're aware of what's going on in school with your peers. Mom has heard from Mrs. Tillison that your work and attitude have improved tremendously; that you've made up your back homework. We're in your corner, and if the pressure gets too great and you need our help, we're here for you. You understand?" Her head was bent when she nodded; tears were filling her eyes.

The waitress came with the orders and Greg said a small grace. She couldn't remember Greg saying grace in a public restaurant unless he was trying to impress someone dining with them. Something had happened to her dad. He had more command about him, and was more in control. She sneaked a look at him; tears were glistening in his eyes. She attacked her food, chewing it hard to keep emotions at bay.

Diners entered and exited. A noisy group of teens entered, some from school. They saw her and were about to send crude comments her way when they saw her father across from her. Cindy was thankful that her dad was with her, in her corner. She was safe from the taunts and felt secure knowing that God and her parents were on her side. What else mattered?

She looked over at Greg. "Thanks Dad," she said softly. "I appreciate what you're doing for me. I don't know why I said those horrid things; I'd never said or thought things like that before. So forgive me, Daddy." Tears were running down her cheeks.

Greg reached over and took her hand and squeezed it. "It's okay sweetie...this too shall pass. We'll emerge stronger and I believe wiser people."

Attendance at Sunday evening service was large, and the success of the convention was still being savored. The offering plates were passed, song service concluded, and Mike was seated on the front pew when Bert remarked, "You who were at the convention heard about the OTR Foundation opening its purse to churches whose pastors are preaching the gospel of salvation and in need of financial help." He paused to let that information sink in before continuing. "Well we applied on behalf of our church as soon as we heard of this foundation. We filled in their application form, sent it, and in yesterday's mail, we received notice that we qualify for one of their grants."

He stopped, looking at his people, waiting for their reaction. It took a moment for it to sink in. When it did, questions poured from mouths like a burst dam.

"You talking about them giving us cash, Pastor?" Bert nodded. "What strings are attached?" asked a skeptic.

"None, only that we fulfill the plan I presented to them when seeking the funding," replied Bert.

"Did you mortgage the building?" laughed another voice.

"You know me better than that Joe," Bert replied. "There are no strings attached, but honesty is demanded. I wrote of plans I had in mind to reach more souls for Christ; strengthen the influence churches once had, with outreach programs that go house to house, finding needs, and offering help to our community.

"We will be conducting a Bible study program after the holidays, inviting all who are interested to attend. The teachers will be well qualified, leaders in their field. We will later add a children's Bible study course after we get underway. Our teachers will be the best money can buy. The OTR Foundation is interested in results, and that is what we intend to produce. Not just numbers, but souls saved and growing in the Lord."

"What does that acronym stand for preacher?" asked Mrs. Massingill.

"Thanks for asking Aggie. It stands for OLD TIME RELIGION."

"Well now, I like that," said Aggie Massingill, and a chorus of approving voices rose up from the congregation.

Bert had to hold up his hand to get his people back on earth. "I've something else to share with you before we move our conversation to the fellowship hall. Alice and I are providing coffee and donuts in appreciation of all of your hard work for the convention.

"This spring Fair Haven will be conducting a tent revival." He stopped. Silence only answered him back. He continued. "This isn't going to be an all work, no results tent revival. We're going to bring in the biggest evangelists on the scene, and singers who are at the top of the charts. We've got our work cut out for us, and I don't expect to do this all by my lonesome. Some of you retirees who can still hobble around—I'm looking to you to help out." Silence again met his words.

Then a gravelly voice broke the stillness. "Yeah, you can count on me preacher; I was saved in a tent revival."

"Me too," came another. "Never will forget that night. I was ten years old...still can feel the spirit." Amens sounded.

The flood gate opened with anecdotes, and closed when Mike interjected that the discussion would continue in the fellowship hall with a cup of coffee and a donut. He prayed. The flock followed the shepherd and staff to the waiting coffee urns.

Getting through to Cindy that her behavior was unacceptable, and that new house rules would be followed or consequences would be paid, was easier than what Greg Hunt was now facing.

He stood at the head of a table in the restaurant's private dining room. He hoped the steaks his friends were enjoying at his expense would mitigate the angst his remarks would engender.

Dessert was in front of the men when Greg arose, cleared his throat, and began his peroration. "While you guys were enjoying steaks, I was eating crow." Eyebrows raised; his words had gotten their attention. They stopped eating; some picked up coffee cups and eyed Greg warily.

He began. "It's no secret I've been pushing to oust Davenport from our pulpit for almost a year. I convinced you guys to see it my way, and you've been loyal to my cause. I didn't tell you before, but my concern was centered around my 16-year-old daughter who was driving us crazy. She'd left Fair Haven to attend Awakening, and I thought the way to bring her back was to become more like that church. I've used every trick in the book to oust Bert, going so far as to freeze church assets while he was out of town. Nothing's worked. Well, call it an epiphany or whatever, but God brought me to my knees the other night, and guess who came to our rescue? You guessed it...Bro. Davenport. His wisdom and help despite my bad behavior really blew me outta the water. He saved my family, and showed me that compromise in the church is not the way to bring our teens closer to God."

Greg took a drink of water; the men noticed that his hand shook. Some sneered; others had empathy. "I'm here tonight to say that instead of working against Bert, from now on, I'm on his side. There you have it. I'm apologizing to you for coercing you into going against the shepherd of the flock. I've made my peace with God; I know it's going to be harder making peace with some of you. But that's the gist of it. I was wrong, and I know I've caused lots of you to go against your better judgment. I ask forgiveness; that's all I can do." Greg stopped and waited for their retaliations.

Several upset voices mumbled against him, that he had deceived them, and upset their wives and family. Matt Johnson furrowed his eyebrows and spoke the loudest. "My wife told me all along this is ridiculous. It's caused a lot of strain between us the past few months."

Jeffry Adams turned the tide, spoke sense. "We're adults. If we'd not been willing, we'd have resisted your cause. Some of us probably had grudges against Bert and you gave us an opportunity to express it openly. I'm glad it's over. Like Matt there, my wife's been unhappy about this situation. But, as far as I'm concerned, I've no hard feelings. I give you credit for having the guts to face us, and level with us about your reason for beginning this fight and why you're putting an end to it. You've got my vote of confidence, whatever that might mean."

They rose as one, none feeling the need for third coffees or even chatting in the parking lot. Each wanted his space. Greg thanked the men and escaped to his car feeling like the stray dog no one wanted around. He was sick in the pit of his stomach. The crow was indigestible; he'd eaten it all, from feathers to scrawny claws. Yet in spite of the indigestion, there was a feeling of exhilaration, that he'd faced his Goliath and hadn't been stoned.

Cindy Hunt's entrance into the classroom that Monday morning was tantamount to the ocean breaking its banks. Mrs. Tillison carried her sack lunch to the staff lounge, ready to entertain her peers by recounting the Cindy Hunt phenomenon that morning. Tillison grinned as she tossed in her quarter for a cup of Bunn coffee in the lounge kitty.

"Don't tell me you had a good morning," drawled Pat Morgan, P.E. instructor. Tillison shook her head and started laughing. Her colleagues chewed food, drank coffee, and waited.

Tillison had the floor; a hush came over the staff. "The first bell had rung; the second was about to ring as this girl came into the classroom. She approached my desk and handed me a stack of papers. 'These are the last of my back assignments,' she said. I almost collapsed. I recognized the voice, but I could hardly tell by looking that it was Cindy Hunt. She was looked like a girl from the 50s, her natural auburn hair was brushed to a sheen, in a smart page boy hairdo. She wore a touch of lipstick, a no-no these days; perish the thought that a girl should look pretty. Instead of her usual skin-tight tattered jeans, Cindy wore elegant tan pants and a white shirt topped with an open-necked brown sweater. She looked so classy. Her outfit shrieked SCHOLAR. I've an idea that that was the picture she wanted to convey. The new Cindy was putting away childish dress and moving toward being a mature adult."

"How'd the kids in the class react?" asked a listener.

Tillison shook her head. "Everyone was frozen in their seats. As she sat down, people finally recognized who it was. After some whispers and raised eyebrows, the class president Toby Williams whistled, stood up and began clapping. 'Way to go, Cindy, at last the female of the species is well represented.' You can say what you please, but regardless of trendy society, a man enjoys looking at a woman who looks female rather than a replica of himself."

"Oh my goodness! What did the girls do?" asked another colleague.

"They were speechless; didn't expect that kind of acceptance from the guys. If I judge the situation right, those girls are going to be wondering how to get that kind of positive attention. They want to please the guys, and by patterning their dress after Cindy they will be putting her back as the trendsetter they'd shoved under the bus."

"Interesting," remarked Ms. Morgan, "I wonder how long this will last? Probably just a stunt."

"Don't think so," said Tillison. "I think Cindy's found satisfaction in becoming her own person, and coming to school to gain knowledge. Sounds corny...but I believe seeking wisdom got her through the past few tough weeks. She won't go back to giving her studies short shrift." The room quieted as the staff mulled over the tale, and eating became a priority as the hands of the clock moved steadily around the dial.

Lisa drove Cindy home that afternoon. "You carried the day Cindy," said Lisa laughing. "You're back on top...you have those girls on their heels, especially the way your new look intrigued the guys. You'll be back leading the pack with them eating out of your hand," she finished dryly.

"I didn't do it for that reason Lisa. You're partly to credit for the change. I followed your advice about setting goals rather getting even. By the time I completed my back homework, I'd set a pattern for studying and getting something out of my lessons. I even did additional research on some related subjects. What I'm wearing today reflects the mood I'm in. Lisa, I really want to be a scholar; knowledge gives me fulfillment. I've my own agenda; my peers don't factor in on my happiness or unhappiness. My looks reflect how I was feeling inside. I like the new me."

Lisa Brown smiled knowingly. "I'm proud of you Cindy. Why not come to our youth rally this Friday night? I'll pick you up. Pastor Davenport's making arrangements for the church to sponsor a tent revival in a couple of months. The youth group from church is going to have a part in planning it. Why not come? Teens from three area churches are meeting with us this Friday. We'll have a great time."

"I'll think about it Lisa, but I won't need a ride." She put her hand in her bag and held up her keys. "Dad gave them back to me a while ago."

"Huh! But, you've been riding the bus–I've seen you."

"Yeah," grinned Cindy. "I didn't have the stomach to start another round of questions about how I got my car back. Wasn't worth the effort. Besides, I'm used to the bus; doesn't bother me now, and it saves me having to hunt a parking spot and spend money on gas. So why give up those goodies to show that I'm driving again?"

Lisa drove off shaking her head and grinning. She was really beginning to like Cindy Hunt; she'd become more down to earth, less fixated on self. For some reason, she thought Cindy just might show up Friday night.

Walking to her front door, Cindy made up her mind that she'd check out the Friday night youth group thing. If she got bored, hey, she could always leave.

CHAPTER TWENTY

The subject of the tent revival was never far from the surface. It was scheduled for the month of May. With Christmas over, January ushered in the beginning of adult Bible studies. The interest was over the top; the renowned theologians were outstanding. The adults met two nights a week in the fellowship hall. Attendance grew every week, and Bert and the staff were excited beyond words.

"Even with all that's going on with our Bible courses," said Bert that Sunday morning in February, "we've not been dragging our feet where the tent revival is concerned. Committees have been established: Tent and chair committee; refreshment committee; nursery committee; lavatory committee; parking lot committee...and the list goes on. Already we've many volunteers but as the event draws nigh we'll need every man who has a hand to lend it to the cause.

"We've located a lot that will accommodate the tent, and be accessible to many areas in our city, and it's near the highway. We will have buses that will pick up people at certain locations and return them to that location after the meeting."

Aggie Massingill got the ball rolling by recounting her experience as a nine-year-old, visiting a revival, and getting saved. "Preacher, I was going on 10 when I got saved at a tent revival. The preacher preached hard on hell and warned us not to go there. When folks began going to the altar, I stepped away from mom and dad and headed to the front. Yeah, it was something. I can still see my mom crying because I got saved." Anecdotes took the floor and Bert had difficulty turning off the reminiscences.

"We need more hellfire and brimstone preaching today," added Jeff. "They say we shouldn't scare people into believing there's a hell. But I scare my kids about booze, drugs, porn, things I don't want them getting into and ruining their lives. Hell's real, so why not warn people, and tell them how to escape it...through Jesus."

Bert ended the meeting on a note of high expectations for the coming tent revival. "There is still plenty to do; committees that are working will be calling on you for support. A list of committees will be in the narthex; please sign up for any committee you're willing to serve on. Those who are physically impaired, we'll have a prayer committee for you. Prayer is our best ally."

Pastor looked at his watch. "Good grief! It's almost 8:30. Time to get home...get those kids to bed and set the alarm clock. Bob, will you close in prayer, please."

Alice, seated across from Bert's desk, sipped coffee and watched him sort out phone messages. She smiled, remembering the years she sat across from him as secretary, loving him from afar. That she should be sitting across from him now as his wife was a miracle brought about by God. George dying; her inheriting his fortune; her marriage to Bert; the revival going on in their church and many other churches...what an unbelievable, mysterious God is our Maker, she mused.

"David called this morning, before I left for the office," she said, getting his attention.

"Oh? Anything up?" asked Bert, prioritizing his messages.

She laughed softly. "The trustees are writing checks nonstop. Rev. Butler's inundated with requests, and almost all applicants are meeting OTR qualifications. David's beginning to take notice, and his interest is piqued."

The phone rang, and she reached for the instrument. "Pastor Davenport's office, how may I help you?"

"Hey, Alice, good to hear your voice. Is your other half around? Hope you're keeping him out of mischief."

Alice shook her head and handed Bert the phone. She mouthed, "Brother Hinton," and Bert nodded.

"How's the tent revival coming along?" boomed Ivo in Bert's ear.

"Please," begged Bert. "I eat, sleep and dream revival. But I'm actually swamped with people wanting to help. Committees are tripping over each other—I guess they think there's a committee of the year award! We rented a huge field that once housed an outdoor theater. Had to tear down the left over structure, level the field, and pour tons of gravel on it. And, we've rented a tent that seats 3,000 plus. Hired buses to pick up folks from outlying districts. We're advertising on every media out there: T.V., social media, radio, Internet, and distributing flyers door to door. We've rented enough potty johns to accommodate an army!"

"Who's the evangelist?" queried Hinton.

"Josiah Templeton."

"Ah, I'm impressed," said Ivo. "He's quite an international star even with millennials. How'd you get him to come?"

"C'mon Hinton...we're paying top dollar for everything with this revival. We met his price. Hope he's worth it."

Hinton laughed. "Yeah, I hear you. He's gregarious, charismatic, but definitely an orthodox Christian with a great following, from young to seniors. Who'd you hire for the music end?"

"Mike will do the congregational singing; he's dependable. The guest musicians and singers are top of the chart entertainers. Lots of country gospel, and traditional and contemporary hymns; no rock, we're not sponsoring a rock revival. And we've got prayer groups going. We'll need every prayer we can send heavenward."

Bert paused, then turned the conversation back to his old friend. "So how about you, Ivo; did you send in an application?"

"You kidding? Of course I did, as soon as I got home. I filled in the little blanks as judiciously as any fair-haired boy hoping for a handout."

"If I'm not being nosy, what're your goals, Ivo?"

"For one thing, we're adding Sunday School rooms for the younger kids and an addition to our youth building. Already got estimates on both projects. My church's come alive, has caught a vision, praise the Lord. Of course knowing that funds are available for these projects definitely adds to their enthusiasm. When—if—we get the grant, I've plenty of visions dancing in my head like Christmas sugar plums. If your tent revival survives, hey, we just might copy your industrious efforts and put up a tent of our own. So you see my brother, much depends on the outcome of your tent revival whether or not revivals spring up all over our Southern posterity."

He heard Bert grunt and laughed. "C'mon you know the old adage, imitation is the greatest form of flattery."

Bert grinned knowingly. After a brief prayer for the revival, they disconnected.

The opening service, 7 p.m., May 19, was heralded via paid media daily: "Revival has come to Safe Haven! Everyone welcome! Dr. Josiah Templeton, international speaker, will bring riveting messages on end time prophecy. Don't miss the country gospel group Harmony Quartet, and Linda Gaskill, the lovely contralto. Tent revival sponsored by Fair Haven Baptist Church, Rev. Robert Davenport, pastor. Refreshments; nursery accommodations. Come one...come all!"

The phone rang incessantly, keeping Alice and Ruth busy answering questions and taking notes for the Pastor. Bert, with too many irons in the fire, stopped long enough to put out the verbal fires rising in intensity among various committees. The parking lot committee was ready to do battle with the porta potty committee over where to put the necessary facilities. The nursery workers were jawing about cut off ages for nursery care. The refreshment committee was in a tizzy about how many snacks each attendee was entitled to. The chair committee found fault in the arrangement of chairs, and on and on it went.

Meanwhile Bert was carrying a hidden anxiety. The evangelist couldn't be reached. His cell was either turned off or the battery was dead; Templeton wasn't answering Bert's increasingly frantic calls.

To top it all off, as the evening approached, the weather forecast showed increasing likelihood of heavy rain for Tuesday evening, opening night. With that ominous prediction, all other concerns went mute. The prayer committee met in earnest that morning. "Lord, Lord, don't let it rain," members implored fervently.

But despite their prayers, at 6 p.m., an hour before the service began, the sky opened and rain came down in proverbial buckets. Bert groaned along with the entire church. Their hard work would be a washout. But the show must go on. The parking lot swallowed up the new gravel and left holes of mud puddles and rain. The churches that had promised to come, came with half-empty buses. A few hardy visitors came in spite of the weather, cautiously parking, and walking through the mud to the tent.

Bert's people were out in full force. The evangelist had finally surfaced from outer space and assured Bert that he'd be there on time. One less worry, breathed Bert thankfully.

Mike led the singing that night; doing his best to enthuse a sodden, cold audience that would have preferred a cup of hot coffee to the bottled water they had been given at entrance. The quartet's joyful notes were drowned out from the noise of the rain and wind; attempts to raise the volume resulted in unpleasant squawks from the sound system. Linda Gaskill attempted but failed to reach notes that this night seemed to escape her range.

An audible sigh was felt when Templeton stood behind the pulpit. It was as if the congregation thought as one: When this guy finishes his spiel, we're outta here. No doubt about it, the weather had nudged the Spirit out of the tent.

Somehow the evangelist's clothes had escaped the ravages of rain that had soaked many in the congregation. However, the torrential rain fell on the roof and drowned out every other word he spoke. The people leaned forward to listen, and some tried lip reading—but their effort was futile in the midst of the downpour. Wind roared through the tent, adding to the discomfort of the people.

Evangelist Templeton stopped screaming his words, and implored Mike to lead the congregation in song until things quieted down. Mike obliged. "Let's sing that old favorite, 'Love Lifted Me.'" Not a good choice. Love fell flat on the lips of a dispirited, damp, annoyed audience. Adding to their discomfort, the strip lights flickered off and on swaying above them like a guillotine ready to fall. Singing did nothing to mitigate the gloom. On and off went the lights as if someone were playing with the light switch. Then, thunder boomed, lightning flashed, and a ferocious wind roared through the tent, circling the terrified congregation. The singing stopped, and Mike stood mute.

Bert heard groans and whimpers. "Oh God," he breathed, "What's going on? Where are You?"

As suddenly as it came, the wind exited with a swoosh. A sudden silence descended as the thunder, lightning, and rain ceased. The tent no longer shook, and the lights came on strong and bright. A feeling of rapturous joy filled the tent; people blinked in the light. A noticeable warmth came upon the gathering.

Bert would say later that the quartet was given a word from God. From their spot on the platform, they broke out in beautiful harmony: "SPIRIT OF THE LIVING GOD, FALL FRESH ON ME. SPIRIT OF THE LIVING GOD, FALL FRESH ON ME. MELT ME, MOLD ME, FILL ME, USE ME...SPIRIT OF THE LIVING GOD, FALL FRESH ON ME."

Evangelist Templeton, tears streaming down his cheeks, splayed his hands to the people. "Truly the Spirit of the Living God has fallen on our gathering tonight. We witnessed the power of the Holy Spirit, that third Person of the Trinity. His office is to lift up Christ; bring men to a saving knowledge of Jesus. People need the Lord. The Spirit is here tonight wooing hearts to God; souls to salvation."

Weeping was followed by feet walking the aisles. Bert and his workers knelt with penitents at the altar. Out of nature's chaos came great conviction; out of conviction came belief. The Spirit fulfilled His office that night. He exalted Christ, convicted men of sin, and wooed them into the Kingdom of God.

They were sipping bedtime decaf when the phone rang. Bert looked at his watch: 10:30 p.m. He sighed wearily and reached for the phone. "Pastor..."

"Bert, it's just me, Mike. Nothing's wrong, just wanted to let you know that our tent revival's hit the Internet. Some that were there have already posted tonight's happenings on social media; you know, Facebook, Twitter and other sites. Who'd of thought our revival would get such coverage? Thousands read those posts...what a way to advertise our revival, for free!"

"You're kidding! And they're saying nice things about us, Mike?"

"Oh yeah; of course, they're talking about that crazy weather and how God just shut it all down. Tonight's one for *Ripley's Believe It or Not*. And thousands of people are going to wake up to posts like this one: 'Well, I met the Holy Ghost tonight. WOW!'...and plenty more like that, all positive. Couldn't believe what I was reading, Bert."

"Well, I'll be," said Bert, sitting up straighter. "I'm not into social media, too technical for an old geezer like me. But if it elicits interest in our revival, that's fantastic. God can use any method He pleases to spread His message! Mike, I should have known that in spite of the weather, God was in control. I panicked, worrying about the people sitting there, cold and miserable; Templeton trying to be heard above the pounding rain on the roof. I cringed for the singers trying valiantly to entertain a congregation too miserable to listen. I complained to God that we were doing this for Him, and where was He? Then He shut off the water works and brought such a sudden peace...my lack of faith hit me in the face. What an outpouring of the Holy Ghost; what an awesome God we serve!"

"Oh yeah, preacher, we experienced a genuine 21st century miracle tonight. Wonder what's in store for us tomorrow? Hope it's not more rain!"

"Well, if God's in it, does it matter? And before I forget, ask Ruthie to call the gravel company and order more truckloads of gravel. That parking lot is a sea of mud."

"Yeah," said Mike. "I'll see to it."

"You did an outstanding job tonight, Mike, keeping that congregation from getting up and walking out."

Mike laughed. "Thanks, Bert. And that thought floated through my mind...the congregation just rising up as one body and moving out of that sodden tent. I could almost read the headlines: 'Congregation walks out on tent revival, preferring the rain.'"

Bert laughed. "Thank goodness God had something else in store!" They said goodnight and disconnected.

CHAPTER TWENTY-ONE

The revival was scheduled to last for two weeks, Tuesday evening through Sunday evening. Midway through the second week, Templeton approached Bert after the service. "There's no way you can shut this revival down Bro. Davenport," Josiah Templeton told him. "I've been in revivals for more years than I care to count, and there's a difference between man-driven and God-driven revivals. God's leading this one. I'm sorry I can't stay to see how God's going to end it, but I've another commitment I can't break."

Bert understood, but agreed with Templeton that he couldn't close a revival that was bringing not only local crowds but also people from neighboring states. God would close the revival in His own time.

The problem now facing them: who would do the work of the evangelist? Templeton's ministry ended Sunday night. Bert voiced his concern to his people. "There's no way we can close the revival with crowds of people still showing up. Dr. Templeton can't stay. We're searching for another evangelist and I'm asking you all to pray that we'll find one of the same caliber as Josiah Templeton. We'll advertise our change in evangelists, and our change in evenings. We'll have services Friday, Saturday, and Sunday nights only, as long as God sees fit to keep us going. This will give us all a breather." The faithful were glad of the much-needed reprieve.

Josiah Templeton came to the rescue. "I just thought of a retired evangelist living in Florida, but he's in his 80s. He retired a couple of years ago, but he's one of the best of the old-time revivalists still with us. I took many a page from his book on evangelism. Don't know his heath situation, but it's worth a phone call to find out."

As soon as Templeton wrote down the phone number, Bert was dialing. As he listened to the ring, ring, ring, of the phone, he realized he didn't know the preacher's name. Bert was discombobulated when a voice answered with, "McKay residence, Stuart McKay speaking."

Bert stammered, relieved. "I was given this number, and told a retired evangelist lived here."

"That's correct, I was an evangelist for over 45 years. Retired 3 years ago. What's your interest in me, sir?"

Bert relaxed, and stated his reason for calling. "I'm Pastor Davenport from Safe Haven, South Carolina. Our church is in the midst of hosting a tent revival, scheduled to last two weeks. But it has generated so much interest that I believe God wants us to continue. Our evangelist can't stay longer than the two week period due to another commitment. We want to find an evangelist dedicated to preaching the old-time gospel, as Dr. Templeton's been doing with tremendous success. It was he who gave me your number. I know you're retired, but would you consider taking on our revival?" Bert held his breath and waited.

After what seemed like an eternity, Stuart McKay was asking questions of Bert. "Is this the revival I've heard about in the news? My wife Millie was just reading about a revival that was getting lots of media attention because of the crowds it was attracting."

Bert laughed. "Yeah, that's the revival I'm calling about. We feel God doesn't want to shut us down. People are coming in droves, hungry for the Word, and there are converts every night." Bert stopped talking to let his words resonate with McKay. Even as he waited, Bert knew McKay was the man God intended to use to continue the revival. He breathed heavily as he waited.

"When d'you want me there," asked McKay, "and for how long?"

"Can you start next Friday night? As for how long—I'm clueless. It's not my call, Dr. McKay, so I can't be specific."

"True, true, well we can discuss terms when I get there. My wife may come, if not now, later on. I don't stay away from home too long these days."

"I understand. We'll have a hotel suite reserved for you, as long as you need it. My office will make arrangements for your flight here when you let us know your itinerary. Thanks Dr. McKay, you've relieved my anxious mind tremendously. Looking forward to meeting you in person. I believe you're the man God had in mind for us."

"We'll see, laddie; we'll see," said the old evangelist in a voice tempered by experience. Dr. Stuart McKay was a Scotsman born in America of Scottish parents. A 5'9" man of stocky build, white headed, with a trim white beard, his appearance was reminiscent of a prophet, sans the long robe. His authoritative voice belied his 83 years; its timbre could mesmerize audiences. Hellfire and brimstone were his favorite subjects. "People need to know they exist," was his comeback when chided for the content of his sermons. He'd retired when churches, once traditional, put perimeters around the subjects he could preach. Rather than preach nonsense, as he dubbed social gospel topics, he hung up his clerical collar and went fishing.

"Mike, I'm satisfied he's the man God had in mind. Alice looked up his bio. Retired 3 years ago after many years in evangelism. He has an earned doctorate; and something he doesn't brag about, is a knighthood from the Queen when he preached in the U.K. years ago."

"I'm impressed. So it's all set that he's coming?" asked Mike.

"All but financial considerations; he said we'd discuss that when he gets here. He'll begin Friday night following Templeton's last Sunday night service. Alice has booked him at a nice hotel where she's stayed before."

"Great, Bert...just hope he'll be able to get back in the saddle. At 83 he's no young colt."

"Mike, if he's God's man, McKay will get the strength he needs from God, not from bottled vitamins." Bert was excited. Mike hoped the pastor wouldn't be disappointed.

The revival made history on two fronts. One, for the interest it generated and the number of conversions coming from it. Two, for the number of protesters gathered nightly, attempting to shut them down with noisy shouting. Roads were blocked leading to the tent; protesters stood holding placards, screaming obscenities as people entered the property. "Those crackpots are preaching hate; scaring people, setting peace back decades," they accused. Protesters were heard yelling, cursing above congregational singing. The police moved them as far from the tent as possible. Unpleasant though it were, it didn't discourage attendance; in fact it heightened interest in the meetings.

Social media posts praising the revival were followed by posts demanding authorities shut the meetings down; the preachers were teaching hate, causing division among the people. "Should run that rotten gang out of our peaceful community," opined some online.

Bert appealed to Bennett. The police captain shook his head sorrowfully. "Can't do anything about the protests. It's their right of free speech; the speech they're trying to deny you of," he said shaking his head. "I'll have a couple of uniforms parked near the tent to ward off any unruly activists."

The quartet had agreed to stay on. Their enthusiasm along with their harmonious voices pleased the audience to no end. That night evangelist McKay took his seat on the platform, and the quartet sang "I'll Fly Away," inviting the congregation to join in the chorus. The tent fairly rocked. The crowd sang as if their tongues had sprouted wings, and the tent was soaring into space. Bert had difficulty keeping tears of thanksgiving from choking him as he joined the singing.

Mike turned the service over to Bert after leading the congregational hymn "At Calvary." Bert introduced Dr. McKay to the people. Amenities dispensed with, Bert took his seat in the front row, and gazed up at the evangelist.

Dr. Stuart McKay stood gazing at the gathering. A ripple of anticipation spread through the crowd. He peered around the tent as if weighing up every individual in it. He raised both arms in the air, lowered his right arm, extended his index finger and said in an ominous voice. "IS YOUR NAME WRITTEN DOWN IN THE BOOK OF LIFE?" Surprise on the faces of the congregation was their answer.

Holding up his Bible, the evangelist continued. "It is written in the book of Revelation these words: 'And I saw a great white throne, and Him that sat upon it, from whose face the earth and the heaven fled away...and I saw the dead, small and great, stand before God; and the books were opened, and another book was opened, which is the book of life: and the dead were judged out of those things which were written in the books according to their works. And the sea gave up the dead which were in it; and death and hell delivered up the dead which were in them: and they were judged every man according to their works.... And whosoever was not found written in the book of life was cast into the lake of fire.'"

"Och aye," said the evangelist, warming to his subject. "We're all headed for the grave. Again I ask each one of you: What book is your name written in? Our deeds are recorded in books...scary isn't it to think things we did are recorded in books for God's perusal. But the book that holds the key to the soul's final destiny is the book of LIFE. Think of the terror you'll feel when you look in that Book of Life and find that your name isn't in it! It's too late to get right with God; you're dead. No place to hide, for everything is open to God: sea, death, hell. God has stretched out His hand to you time and time again, but you've rejected His Son the Lord Jesus. Now you stand before the Great White Throne where God is seated. When you look in the Lamb's Book of Life, will you find your name there, or will it be missing from the line it should have been on? God is not willing that any should perish. Your soul's destiny is in your hands. You are still alive...you still have time to make it right with God. 'Choose ye this day whom ye will serve...as for me and my house, we will serve the Lord!' It is still day...come to the Savior now! Grace ceases when death enters the body."

A loud commotion rose when several people scattered among the audience stood up shouting, "Hate monger! Scaring people into believing your rubbish! Don't listen to this man!"

Bert was instantly on his cell dialing Bennett.

Stuart McKay raised both hands to heaven and shouted, "My people get away from those cretins lest you be stricken when God's wrath falls upon them!" The worshippers hastened away from the agitators. Turning to the protestors, McKay pointed his right index finger at them, and boomed: "COME OUT OF THEM YE DEVILS, COME OUT OF THEM YE DEMONS, IN THE NAME OF JESUS THE SON OF GOD, COME OUT OF THEM, COME OUT OF THEM...YE DEVILS...OUT, OUT, OUT, IN THE NAME OF CHRIST, COME OUT!" The lights flickered off and on, and began to sway back and forth. A silence fell so thick that even the sound of breathing was muted. McKay's words echoed round and round the tent.

The agitators were dumbstruck, looking frantically at one another and backing away from the awesome figure on the platform. When they reached the entrance, they bolted in terror. Bennett's men met them as they fled and arrested them for trespassing.

A round of applause broke the tension. People hugged one another; they'd witnessed God's man in action, with the Spirit working the lights.

Stuart McKay mopped his brow and grinned at his audience. "Och aye, God knows how to deal with the devil's own. Now how about it... where will you spend eternity? Is your name written down? Mike how about singing 'Just as I Am.' It's a song that brings tears to my heart, and once it brought conviction to my soul. Come just as you are to the foot of the Cross. The Lord receives all who come."

The soul-rending song brought conviction; scores of people made their way to the altar seeking forgiveness for their sins from the Lord, while others opened their hearts to Jesus Christ.

Bert breathed a prayer of thanksgiving. McKay had been anointed that night by the Holy Spirit. Bert sensed the moment when the Spirit stepped into the shoes of Stuart McKay and spoke through him. Bert had heard of such phenomena occurring; tonight he'd seen and heard it.

McKay was kneeling beside weeping penitents at the altar. Bert and his counselors followed with open Bibles, leading people down the gospel pathway to Christ.

Mike, tears running down his cheeks switched to PASS ME NOT OH GENTLE SVAIOR...HEAR MY HUMBLE CRY...WHILE ON OTHERS THOU ARE CALLING...DO NOT PASS ME BY.

Bert saw but hardly recognized a man as he staggered to the altar and fell on his knees. It was Greg Hunt, trembling, tears streaming down his cheeks. Bert's heart broke with compassion. He waited a moment before kneeling beside Greg; gently putting an arm around his shoulders. Bert was silent, but Greg recognized his person and whispered so quietly Bert had to lean closer to hear him. "Pastor, until tonight I thought I was saved. But I realize God's Spirit wasn't in me. My belief stopped at my head; never reached my heart. My faith was academic not spiritual. I want to be saved Bert."

Pastor nodded and led Greg to salvation reciting Paul's words to the Romans. "If thou shalt confess with thy mouth the Lord Jesus, and shalt believe in thine heart that God hath raised Him from the dead, thou shalt be saved. For with the heart man believeth unto righteousness, and with the mouth confession is made unto salvation."

"Greg, do you believe that Jesus is the Son of God, that He died for your sins, and do you accept Him as your Savior?"

Without hesitation Greg Hunt whispered, "Oh, yes, yes...I believe and want Jesus to come into my heart." Bert followed the confession with a brief prayer, and Greg convulsed into tears. "What I've missed all these years, assuming, but not knowing Christ as Savior." A figure joined Greg at his other side.

"Daddy, daddy, I'm so happy you're here." Cindy was kneeling beside her father, arms round his neck. Bert moved away...this was not a moment to intrude.

The evangelist sipped tea and toyed with the food Alice had prepared for them. They were tired; it was 10:30. The service had ended an hour before. Each was revisiting silently the events of that fantastic meeting.

Alice broke the silence by exulting over the number of people being saved that night. The weary Stuart McKay nodded. "Och aye, lass. Heavenly angels had plenty to rejoice over tonight, with all those souls making reservations for heaven. God is merciful. He doesn't want anyone to go to the place He prepared for the devil and his angels. And to think He used an old codger like me to preach that message, and honor it with His Spirit. Oh He used my old bones tonight and filled my mouth with words I'd not intended to use. How the Holy Ghost took care of those bent on causing mischief. Every person in that tent will remember till the day they die, how those would-be agitators ran from the tent tonight!" He laughed remembering the scared look on the faces of the protestors as they backed out of the tent. "They won't be back," he predicted.

McKay wiped his eyes with his cloth napkin, and took refuge from built-up emotions by tackling the food before him.

"Brother Bert, I've been doing lots of soul searching in retirement. I left evangelism, fed up with changes taking place in traditional churches. Fed up listening to orthodox clergymen excusing their departure from gospel preaching to preaching social twaddle. The day I was informed that I had to watch what I preached and how I preached it, lest I offend delicate ears of the congregation, was the day I hung up my clerical collar.

"And, I was also struggling against being judgmental about the converts these modern churches were claiming to have. My concern: were the conversions real or imagined? I don't like playing judge, for only God can look into a man's heart and know its condition. But it bothered me. What if people thought they were saved and weren't?

"I grew up in an age when going to church meant coming into a sanctuary where organ music played, setting the mood for worshipping God. I still like that atmosphere. The focus was on God. 'For the Lord is in His Holy temple; let all the earth keep silent before Him.' An ambience of reverence was present. These new churches focus on people. Messages attendees want to hear; music they want to sing. God is given short-shrift in His holy temple. Many new age pastors replace the Holy Spirit for worldly gadgets, in order to entice people into their churches."

The old evangelist lifted his tea cup to his lips, grimaced, and was about to put it on the saucer when Alice took it from him. She returned shortly with a fresh cup of steaming Earl Grey tea. He grinned at her and said, "Thanks, bonnie lass." She smiled and nodded.

"Well," continued McKay, "to get back to my meandering. The other night I was reading for the umpteenth time what John had to say about the Holy Spirit, in John 16." Stuart rummaged in his jacket pocket, and brought out a tattered copy of the New Testament. He flipped pages, found his verses and commenced to read. "Jesus, speaking to His disciples said, Howbeit when He, the Spirit of truth, is come, He will guide you into all truth: for He shall not speak of himself; but whatsoever He shall hear, that shall He speak: and He will shew you things to come. He shall glorify Me: for He shall receive of mine, and shall shew it unto you."

McKay cleared his throat, leaned a little forward and said, "Now, I'd read those verses even before I wore long pants. But, the other night the Spirit rubbed my nose in them. 'Stuart, do you not ken...it doesn't matter to me where the gospel's preached. It could be in a shack, or a bar where a juke box is blaring away; or in a sanctuary where organ music's playing. I'm listening for words spoken about Christ. And, WHATSOEVER I HEAR, I take and magnify Christ. It's the gospel I'm listening for. It's the gospel that convicts and converts sinners. The controversy splitting churches is Satan's diversionary tactic. Pastors caught up in 21st century changes are giving less time to preaching Christ, and more time to social issues. Your calling, Stuart, is to preach the Word. Don't waste your time fighting worldly things; fight to make sure the gospel isn't stifled into silence.'"

"Bro. Davenport, that wee talk with the Spirit changed directions for me. I'm dusting off my collar and getting back on my pony, riding the range with the Word wherever the Spirit leads. This revival's of God. You've been blessed; souls have been saved, and I've been rejuvenated. I'll preach wherever I'm called; get around the roadblocks and preach the gospel till God calls me home."

He stood, then took Alice's hand and bent over it and said sincerely, "Thanks for your wonderful hospitality. And, I understand it was you that made reservations for my comfort in that lovely hotel suite. Best accommodations I've ever been privileged to have away from home." He added softly, "Would you believe me if I told you I once was billeted in a hotel where the bed had a straw mattress?" He laughed at the look of incredulity on her face.

Bert drove him to the hotel; the doorman opened the car door. Bert left the driver's seat to bid the old evangelist goodnight. "You've been a great blessing to me, Bro. McKay. And, thanks for sharing the wisdom you've gathered from the Holy Spirit with me. It has helped wash away the same questions I had about conversions from new age preaching. We forget we're not the potter, only the clay. I look forward to meeting your wife when she comes this week."

"Och aye, you've got a treat coming. Millie's one of a kind." He laughed, t h en said soberly, "Brother Davenport, I've a wee confession to make. I know where the Holy Spirit's coming from, but personally, I still think we ought to include dignity when we worship God in any setting. My opinion!" He winked, shook Bert's hand and followed the doorman into the hotel. Bert waited till the door closed behind them and shook his head, then chuckled. "Yeah, I hear you McKay...I also am of the same opinion still."

EPILOGUE

At 5:30 p.m. cars trickled into the parking lot; by 6:00, cars streamed in; by 6:15 parking spaces were scarce. At 7 p.m., a harried attendant waved cars away as he shut the gate of Redeemer Baptist Church's parking lot in Savannah, Georgia.

Bert and Alice had followed Dr. and Mrs. Ivo Hinton to the Baptist convention. They had arrived in plenty of time to secure good parking spots. They found a pew with a good view of the platform. Miriam and Alice left their seats in search of the ladies, while the men talked and visited with other colleagues who'd arrived early. Ivo Hinton, president ministers' association that year and a favorite of the crowd, was the center of attention. Bert enjoyed listening to the repartee swirling around him, glad that he had Alice to accompany him. Hinton was protesting, "Guys, let's save the questions till the meeting's started, save me from having to repeat myself."

After a short time, Miriam and Alice were back; the men moved to let the women take seats beside their husbands. Soft strains were coming from the piano, a sign that things were beginning to line up for the opening of the convention.

"Ladies and gentlemen, we're about to start our annual spring convention. Please be seated, so that others entering will be able to find seats." The voice belonged to a tall, lanky man in his fifties, adjusting the horned rim glasses that kept sliding down his nose. His suit was navy; shirt, white; tie, red.

"Rev. Simons, from Atlanta," Hinton informed them.

Simons' request was ignored by half the preachers. A shorter, ample girthed man joined Simons on the platform. His sartorial appearance oozed money; his voice, power. He cleared his throat, took the microphone, and said authoritatively, "I saw Brother Bill Copeland in the auditorium a minute ago...Bill where are you?" The cacophony of voices ceased. A hand shot up. "Ah, Bro. Copeland, please open our convention in prayer."

While Rev. Copeland prayed, ministers sneaked to their seats.

"Dear God," prayed Copeland, "we beseech Your presence and blessings on our meeting. Thank you for hearing our prayers. In Jesus name we pray, Amen."

"Thank you, Brother Bill," said the preacher who'd chased the errant to their seats. "Redeemer Baptist Church welcomes each one of you. Our church is here to make sure that you'll have little to gripe about when you leave us." Laughter. "If you need accommodations, see Mrs. Alec Jameson; she and her committee members will be in the narthex at the close of tonight's service. The bulletin you found on your seat delineates the services our people have made available for your comfort. We trust that our convention will be a memorable one to you all."

"For newcomers, I am Dr. Horace Mann, pastor of Redeemer Baptist." Turning to a young man on the platform, he said, "This is Bill Williams, the best song leader in the State of Georgia." He clapped his hand on Williams' shoulder, patted it, and left the platform.

Bill Williams' voice mocked the leanness of his frame; it was strong, vibrant, and resonant. "Turn with me to page 332, 'Standing on the Promises of God.' Please stand. It's oxymoronic to sit while singing about standing." A titter of laughter followed the tired joke. The ministers sang with conviction their belief in the promises of God. The ambience of hope, love, and faith was palpable. Some clergy had ventured to stand on promises and found the foundation, indeed, solid rock. New verve was in the air. New vigor brought about by a foundation that listened to their needs and sent the means by which to accomplish their stated goals.

Bert looked at Alice and winked; she smiled knowingly and nodded. The effect of OTR was on display. Preachers had found their second wind and were glad to be there to share anecdotes.

Protocol followed: offering plates; announcements; prayer requests; recognition of special and first-time guests. A soloist sang an unfamiliar song which yielded polite applause. A male quartet had the clergy on its feet joining in the chorus of "I'll Fly Away."

Again Dr. Mann was speaking from his pulpit. "Since our last convention monumental changes have taken place in some of our churches. At that time, Dr. Hinton introduced us to the OTR Foundation and outlined its mission and its goals. Unbelievable though it sounded, many of us filled out applications and applied despite our inward doubts. At this convention we will hear from some who applied and are tasting the manna God dropped on discouraged preachers. I turn the meeting over to our president, Dr. Ivo Hinton." Horace Mann handed the mike over to Hinton as he mounted the steps to the platform. They shook hands. Mann left the platform, and Hinton stood behind the pulpit, a satisfied smile on his face.

"Great crowd, great spirit; it's so good to be here. Now without wasting any further time, I want to introduce the pastor who hosted that last convention. A recipient of an OTR grant, he will keep you glued to your seats as he describes his church's experiences. I'm speaking of Rev. Bert Davenport, of Safe Haven, South Carolina. He's a shy man, but not too shy, for he boldly proposed and won the hand of lovely Alice. I had the privilege of marrying them a few months ago. C'mon up Bert...I'll quit palavering and give you more time to wax eloquently about the things God's been doing in your neck of the woods. Please welcome Rev. Davenport."

The congregation was on its feet as Bert mounted the three steps to the platform. Alice wiped tears of happiness from her face. It had been a long time since Bert had received accolades from anyone. She listened proudly as he began speaking.

"Thanks for the glad hand, but seriously, I can't take credit for what God did at our tent revival. Like those who heard about OTR, I applied, was accepted, and followed up with the plan I'd outlined on my application: to conduct a city-wide tent revival. We advertised through all available media, and really got the word out to the community. I was so fortunate to have a great team of volunteers who pitched in to cover everything from music to potty johns. But there was one thing no number of committees could control. An hour before the service, the sky opened up and absolutely drenched our grand event." Laughter.

Bert stopped for a sip of water, briefly gauging the audience's engagement with his words. Finding that he had their complete attention, he continued. "It rained, thundered, lightning flashed across the sky. A wind shook the tent. People that had braved the storm sat in abject misery...

clothes damp, clutching the bottled water we'd passed out to everyone entering. I know they'd have gladly exchanged it for a cup of hot coffee." Bert had his audience in stitches as he continued painting the picture of drenched congregants in a swaying tent that threatened to go skyward at any moment.

"Dr. Josiah Templeton, our evangelist, was superb, and tried to reassure me. 'Brother Bert, God's in this...it'll work out.' I confess Romans 8:28 was not what I was thinking at that juncture. As he was trying to preach, the wind sounded like a rushing train swooshing through the tent, and the lights began flickering off, on; off, on; off, on. They were swaying like a guillotine over our heads. By that time, I'd taken up Job's lament, 'Why are you doing this to me, God?'" Laughter and applause broke out.

Bert continued rolling. "The flickering lights went off and stayed off. Thunder shook the tent, lightning cracked, and the wind roared. We sat helplessly, in total darkness. I was praying like never before. Suddenly, the rain stopped beating the roof; the thunder shut up; lightning vanished, and the wind quieted. The silence that followed was intense...it hurt our ears. The lights came on, and warmth like the noonday sun flooded the tent. People began to dry out, and wonders of wonders, reached for their bottled water." Laughter.

"Dr. Templeton raised his arms and shouted that the Holy Spirit had visited us that night. People suddenly began to weep and were headed to the alter without an invitation. Templeton knelt by the pulpit with tears streaming down his cheeks. Almost 90 people confessed Christ as Savior that night. It was an awesome night; an awesome display of the power of the Holy Ghost, the Third Person of the Triune God.

"Social media was awash with posts from people who'd been at the meeting. Thousands read about that incredible night. Needless to say, we filled the tent the next night; people hoping to see the Holy Spirit in action. The Spirit manifested Himself in other ways, but not as He had that stormy night."

"How long did the revival last?" interrupted a voice from the back of the auditorium.

Bert, caught slightly off-guard by the interruption, answered, "We'd planned for a two-week revival; it lasted almost four months."

"Same evangelist?" queried another voice.

"No," said Bert resigned to follow interest rather than fight it. "Dr. Templeton had other commitments; we enticed Dr. Stuart McKay out of retirement. He was with us to the close of the revival."

"Stuart McKay?" said an incredulous voice. "I heard him when I was in high school; all fire and brimstone."

"The same," said Bert dryly. "Still is the best in the business, for all of his 83 years."

Bert knew from years of experience, that getting back to his message wasn't going to happen. He shrugged and let the ministers have their way.

"How many converts did you finally end up with, Bro Bert?"

"Last count, 2,098." A brief silence followed as the number sunk in.

"Did you have any protesters show up?"

"Oh yes. After media postings, they tried to block roads to the tent; surrounded it holding obscene placards. We were peddling hate; should be jailed for racism, hate speech...the canned litany of the uninformed. The police kept them as far from the tent as possible. But a few of them were bold enough to pretend to be worshippers and then disrupted Dr. McKay's sermon. Right in the middle of service, they stood up and challenged him."

"What happened?"

Bert laughed before answering. "McKay may be old, but he's not short on knowing how to tweak liberals. He held his arms up in the air and said, 'My people, get away from these people lest the wrath of God touches you as it destroys them.' Then he pointed at them and bellowed, 'Come out from them ye demons; in the name of Jesus Christ, I command you to come out of these demented protestors!'"

"They really became unhinged then. They wanted to run out of there, but were afraid to turn their back to McKay, lest he zap them. They were a pitiful sight. They backed all the way to the tent entrance, bolted out of the tent right to the arriving police. They spent the night in jail for trespassing."

Bert grinned, adding, "Best of all, that entire event was posted on social media. Needless to say, we had no more inside demonstrators."

"How did the revival end?"

"That was something McKay and I discussed, and prayed about. Interest was still high; souls still being saved; but weariness had crept in. McKay was tiring, my people were exhausted, and the weather getting colder. We decided to tell the congregation that the tent revival would close on the following weekend. I had twinges of regret, but I wanted to make sure we were ending on a high note and I felt the Spirit leading. Once committed, we had peace about it, and so did our wonderful parishioners."

"You planning another revival in the fall?"

Bert sipped water as he considered his answer. "I'm not sure what we'll be involved in, but we're amenable to whatever God has in store for our church. We're already involved in a city-wide Bible study program. Adult classes meet two nights a week; children's classes meet two afternoons a week. We've hired the best Bible teachers in the country. The programs have generated more interest than I'd ever imagined them doing. People want to understand the Bible. Our goal is to teach Christians how to rightly divide the Word of truth; and how to recognize truth from fallacy. And to disciple Christians so that they in turn can disciple others. We believe that morality and knowledge of God's Word go hand in hand. 'Thy Word have I hid in mine heart that I might not sin against Thee.'"

"Bro. Bert, what about that numerologist who posted a date for the end of the world. Where was he coming from?"

Bert shrugged. "Numerology's never been my passion. As for when the end time is, only God knows. Our job is to occupy, be busy in His vineyard, and look for signs of His coming."

A young minister in the front pew raised his hand; Bert acknowledged him. "I'm Jim Nicholson, a recent seminary graduate. I got precious little teaching on end-time prophecy. Would you mind going over end time signs we're to look for?"

Bert glanced at his watch; his allotted time was up. He glanced at Hinton for instruction. Ivo shrugged, so Bert proceeded.

Bert flipped through the New Testament. "Jesus lists signs to look for in Matthew 24. He begins with an analogy of the fig tree. When it buds it's a sign that Spring is coming soon. When we see certain signs Christ refers to, the end time is near. Christ delineated signs: wars, rumors of wars; nation rising against nation; kingdom against kingdom; famines, pestilences, earthquakes, disobedient children, licentious lifestyles; falling away from the faith; lawlessness; increase in knowledge. Jesus said all are the beginning of sorrows.

"Concerning Christians in that day, Jesus states, 'Then they will deliver you up to tribulation and kill you; you will be hated by all nations for My name's sake. Many will be offended and betray one another. False prophets will arise and deceive many...the gospel of the kingdom will be preached in all the world as a witness to all the nations of the world, and then the end will come.'"

Bert continued. "The prophets predicted that Israel would become a nation before the end time. In 1948 the world witnessed that phenomenon when Israel was given statehood by the UN. Not since 586 B.C., when Israel was taken into captivity by the Babylonian Empire, had Israel been a sovereign nation. In May 1948 that all changed; Israel came into possession of the land of Palestine God promised them in the Abrahamic covenant."

"What's the latest on the rebuilding of the third temple?" asked Rev. Joshua Clements.

Bert looked for help from the brethren. "Anyone up to date in temple building?" he asked.

Hinton was on his feet. "Let's deal with the temple after dinner—I believe it is ready." A sigh of relief came from Bert as he descended the platform, amidst applause, and made his way to Alice, sliding in beside her.

She took his hand and whispered in his ear, "You were wonderful, darling...I'm so proud of you." Bert flushed with pleasure. He hadn't finished his speech, but who'd miss what he hadn't said? He was tired, ready to sit down, have a cup of coffee and eat whatever food was placed before him.

While the men gathered in the sanctuary to discuss the rise of the 3rd temple, the women went shopping to take care of the physical temple. They'd been good listeners all day; it was their time now to relax. By the time they returned with things they didn't need their men had discussed the importance of building the third temple.

Jews believe that when the third temple is built, the Messiah will return. Everything needed for temple worship is made and in storage; every implement needed for animal sacrifice, made and stored. Priests' garments measured and stored by the thousands. High priests' miter and robe...made and stored. Musical instruments from the time of David fashioned and stored. Even the cornerstone of the third temple is ready. The red heifer for purifying purposes is bred in Israel. The Sanhedrin disbanded in 400

A.D., but is now an entity as of 2004 A.D. Its function is to purify the temple and everything pertaining to Mosaic law.

"What about the Temple Mount, it's already occupied by the Dome of the Rock," insisted a preacher dedicated to getting things in proper perspective.

"Haven't a clue," admitted unflappable Horace Mann, "but when the time's ready for the Temple to go up, God has great earth moving techniques." Laughter.

The meeting adjourned for the day. All were tired; all were excited. Getting together, exchanging plans and dreams, prompted even the laziest preacher to pick up the shovel and get something moving.

Tuesday was given over to show and tell. Like kindergartners, ministers brought narrative and DVDs to the platform to demonstrate what their church had accomplished with OTR grants. Accomplishments ran the gamut: adding a youth director, painting Sunday school rooms, replacing obsolete baby cribs and toys, adding staff, starting radio programs, and undertaking a stronger counseling ministry. All agreed that the grants had increased enthusiasm and confidence within their churches.

One preacher grinned as he told his church tale. "We bought a new—well, actually a second hand—piano. I noticed our pianist was crying as she played for the morning service. I asked her after service why she'd been crying. 'Pastor,' she said sheepishly, 'it had been so long since I hit keys that weren't duds, and keys that weren't out of tune, that I was overcome by the melodious beauty of the hymns.'"

Bert's testimony of the success of their revival had its desired effect: other pastors could hardly wait to get back home and start putting dates on the calendar for their own event.

They said their goodbyes to the brethren. Bert and Alice thanked Dr. Mann for his people's hospitality. "Wonderful meeting Dr. Mann," enthused Bert on Tuesday night. Rising early Wednesday morning, Alice and Bert were on their way home by 8 a.m.

After a leisurely drive, stopping for breakfast and lunch, they were home by early afternoon. Bert phoned the church for any urgencies that might have arisen in his absence. "No, Pastor," said Ruth. "Everything's fine here. Relax...you're probably worn out." After emptying suitcases and cleaning out the car, Bert was relaxing in his recliner, dozing off. Alice was lying down in their bedroom. Peace cometh to the weary; they were weary.

Late that afternoon the doorbell rang. Bert listened from his study as Alice greeted whomever was at the door. Hearing familiar voices, Bert sauntered to the foyer to find Alice, Mike, and Ruth. "Well, and what brings you two here without the kids? Finally running away from home?"

"That's a thought you shouldn't have put in my head," said Mike brightly. "Nah, Ruthie and I are on a date. Her mom's spending a couple of days with us; her idea. We're gonna take in a movie after we eat. Just stopped by to say hi."

Ruth raised her eyebrows at Mike.

"What's up, Ruthie?" asked Bert, sensing conflict.

She looked at Mike, who blushed. "You going to tell them, or do I?"

Mike shrugged then blurted out, "We're going to have a new church member in a few months," he announced, looking at Ruth. She grinned and nodded her head.

"Oh?" said Bert, not quite comprehending. "Sounds good. Male or female?"

"Don't know, yet," confessed Mike.

It was Alice who saw through the charade. "Oh my goodness, you're going to have a baby!" she exclaimed.

Ruth laughed. "Yes, that's what he's trying to say, we're going to have another baby. It's too soon to tell its gender, only that it's going to be a baby."

"Well," said Bert, "I'm sure you're hoping for a girl this time, seeing you have three boys."

"Oh yeah," said Mike with aplomb. "I told Ruth if it's another boy, I'm leaving them both at the hospital."

Bert laughed uproariously. "That'll be the day, that'll be the day!"

Bert prayed for Ruth and for Mike; for their testimonies, and for God's watch care over the unborn child in the womb. Mike and Ruth left hand in hand. Bert and Alice stood watching their car back out of the driveway.

Turning to Alice, he drew her closer to him. "Honey it's folk like Mike and Ruth bringing babies into the world and teaching them about Jesus, that's kept Christianity alive for millennia. Christianity will never die;

God will always have His remnant to carry on the message of salvation to a lost and dying world." Alice nodded and snuggled closer in his arms.

"You know what honey?" Bert said suddenly.

Alice looked up at him. "What, dear?"

"I'm hungry," said her spouse.

She laughed and shook her head. "And do you know what will never die out, Rev. Davenport?"

He looked quizzically at her. "What?"

"BAPTISTS! For Baptists like to EAT!"

Printed in the United States
By Bookmasters